STUDENT PARTICIPATION IN
DECISION MAKING IN GRADUATE SCHOOLS
OF SOCIAL WORK AND IN
HIGHER EDUCATION

STUDENT PARTICIPATION IN DECISION MAKING

in
Graduate Schools
of Social Work and
in Higher Education

Edited by
PATRICIA J. STICKNEY

COUNCIL ON SOCIAL WORK EDUCATION
345 East 46th St.   New York, N.Y. 10017

FOREWORD

THE COUNCIL on Social Work Education takes great pleasure in presenting *Student Participation in Decision Making in Graduate Schools of Social Work and in Higher Education.* This volume includes diverse articles presenting various points of view on the subject of student participation in decision making. Many noteworthy educators in social work and other branches of higher education are represented in the contents. An extensive annotated bibliography on student participation is also included, and it will provide a useful guide to the literature in this field.

We are sure that the ideas expressed in this volume will be of interest and use to educators and students involved in undergraduate and graduate social work education, and we hope that readers will be stimulated and challenged to think more deeply about this subject.

Sincere thanks are given to Patricia J. Stickney for gathering together the important articles in this field and for her time and effort in compiling the annotated bibliography.

March, 1972

LILIAN RIPPLE
Acting Executive Director

v

TABLE OF CONTENTS

STUDENT PARTICIPATION IN DECISION MAKING IN HIGHER EDUCATION

INTRODUCTION:
AN OVERVIEW, ANALYSIS,
AND INTERPRETATION

IN ORDER TO PROVIDE an overview (which is necessarily selective), I shall initially highlight some of the main content elements found in the diverse articles included within this illuminating and provocative monograph.

Articles in Part I, "General Issues Regarding Student Rights and Responsibilities," are concerned with the practices and issues centering around student participation in the development of policy, procedures designed to safeguard assessment of student performance and control the release of information regarding students, and the handling of student grievances. The treatment of these topics is largely descriptive. It is noted by the authors that formal mechanisms for student participation in policy making are quite new in most of the schools of social work.

In Part II, "Student Participation in Decision Making in Schools of Social Work and in Higher Education," different positions are taken and major ideas and topics are addressed by the various authors.

In Paul Schreiber's article, "Student Involvement in Administration and Policy Formation and in Educational Programs and Curriculum Development," recognition is given that meaningful student participation must take place (at least in most institutions) within the limitations of administrative and faculty accountability, with due regard for the fact that many aspects of a school's operation are subject to ultimate decision making at a higher level within the university and even by bodies outside of it.

The educational rationale for student involvement, with particular emphasis on how student participation in various aspects of policy making can enrich the educational experiences, is emphasized by Winifred Bell, in "Educational Bases for Student Involvement in the Administration of Social Work Schools."

An argument, advanced by Frank Peirce in "Student Involvement: Participatory Democracy or Adult Socialization," is that relatively little has been done thus far—at least in schools of social work—to develop clarity as to the roles, authority, and responsibilities of the various school constitu-

1

encies, particularly students. Also, it is contended that disproportionate emphasis has been put on the limitations and problems of student participation rather than on its potentials and possibilities. Too often, it is claimed, students in schools of social work are seen not as responsible participants but rather as "potential recruits" to be molded into the existing professional pattern.

In "Student Participation in Decision Making in Schools of Social Work," Joseph Vigilante takes note of the fact that the role of students in the decision-making process has been gaining strength in the past several years and that this process is, in reality, a sharing of power within the organizational structure of social work education. He also contends that this process is significantly related to, and influenced by, the current "social revolutions" in society, including the "black revolution" and the "student revolution." These changes, it is said, have met with a good deal of acceptance on the part of social work educators.

Some of the elements in the process of including students in policy making in a given school are described by Lillian Lampkin and Phyllis Caroff in "Faculty, Students, Administration, and Decision Making: An Experience in Interdependence." It is noted in this article that faculty decisions to involve students in various ways were often arrived at under considerable pressure and were, in a sense, highly political. Some of the general principles the authors advance are that responsible power-sharing requires accountability and the integration of change with continuity. They also caution that there should be no hardening of lines between the various constituencies, and that reason must prevail. The empirical experience in the school being described, as reported by the authors, was that the student participation at the level of curriculum planning and policy making proved to be very useful, but that student participation in the implementation of curriculum decisions, such as those matters concerning course content, etc., proved to be rather dysfunctional.

A student perspective, presented by Edward Swanson in "Student Involvement in the Governance of Schools of Social Work: Implications for Social Work Education and Practice," is that heightened student activity is a response to dissatisfactions, both with the educational experience and with the broader society. The basic thesis is that more and more students are expecting to learn how to change institutions and are finding that they have to start with the schools of social work. He places a good deal of emphasis on the limitations of that type of participation which involves collaboration with faculty and administrative personnel on joint bodies. He also notes that conflict can have real value, and that there are significant differences in the experiences of the student body and the faculty, and that these result in different perspectives and interests.

A position argued by Kingman Brewster, Jr., in "The Politics of Academia," is that participatory democracy is often an illusion in many academic and financial decisions and that this is necessarily the case. Hence, he contends that the broad sharing of responsibility for ultimate academic decisions ought not to be the primary thrust of useful university reform; the emphasis should instead be placed on accountability.

In "The Structure of Universities" by Charles Frankel, the basic question is raised as to whether democratic principles require the establishment of "student power" in higher education? In fact, he asks, do such principles even apply to institutions of learning in the same sense that they do in the political arena? In other words, are colleges and universities sufficently like cities, national governments, unions, or factories to justify the use of the same political arguments in relation to them? Frankel reasons that they are so different that another set of principles applies to them. He contends that there is only a limited relationship to what might be called "class conflict" in the university, and that the employer-employee model does not fit. In like manner, he contends that the student cannot be said to be exploited in the sense that the term is commonly used in other sectors of society. He also places a good deal of emphasis on the special role of expertise and the need for particular types of competence in academic decision making. His essential conclusion is that the case for student participation in policy making cannot be argued from the point of view of protection against tyranny and oppression, or on the basis of fundamental rights. It must to be justified on other grounds, such as educational ones, if such justification is to be convincing.

The arguments for and against student participation are presented in "For and Against Student Participation" by Earl McGrath. The pro arguments he lists are:
a. the contrasts between institutional professions and actions
b. the sophistication of today's students
c. the need to educate students in democratic living
d. the contributions students could make to improve higher education
e. the abolition of the doctrine of *in loco parentis*
f. the improvement of instruction.

The objections to student participation are summarized as follows:
a. students will dominate the academic society
b. the immaturity of students
c. the brief involvement of students
d. ignorance of professional values
e. interference with study and gainful employment.

The thesis advanced by Fred Kerlinger in "Student Participation in University Educational Decision Making" is that educational policy-making is, and should be, exclusively a faculty function in the ultimate sense, although students can and should participate in aspects of the decision-making process.

Jay Schaffer, however, takes the justification for student participation

3

as a given, and in "Students in the Policy Process" he focuses on an exploration of the implications of actually admitting students to the policy process.

Bruce Johnstone, in "The Student and his Power," suggests that rather than the usual structure of shared decision-making we should think in terms of student power through various models of informal, indirect, and "lower level" participation, such as consumer preferences, lower-level communications (at the departmental or course level), etc.

"Student Participation in Curriculum Planning and Evaluation" by Carl Slater presents a discussion of student participation in decision making as particularly related to curriculum planning in medical schools.

These, then, are some of the major positions advanced and issues and topics discussed in the various articles contained in the monograph.

The publication of this monograph is itself a testimonial to the belief that the dynamics of history and the momentum of trends, while limiting the range of alternatives, do not preclude significant choices and reasonable decision making, even in an area such as governance. It is in this spirit, that I shall examine certain core ideas which appear to be basic to judgments about governance procedures and which have a decided bearing on a number of the points identified above.

The first of these concerns the nature of the educational experience. The pursuit of knowledge and the learner-teacher relationship are unlike a marketplace transaction in at least the following respects:

1. The knowledge the student wishes to acquire is not a scarce resource. In this sense, then, the student's gain in terms of knowledge is not a loss either to the instructor or to other students. Thus, the awarding or a given grade, such as an A, by the instructor does not deprive that instructor of a portion of a limited fund of A's which he possesses. It is true, of course, that in certain situations an instructor may be under pressure not to award too many high grades nor too many low grades because this will be felt to reflect on his standards or his qualities as a teacher. In theory, however, the optimum situation would be for an instructor to be so successful in his teaching that he brought every student up to the "A level." Hence, even when certain realities, such as those mentioned above, influence the actual distribution of grades, there is no *inherent* conflict of interest between the instructor and the student in relation to the desired end. This is an absolutely essential distinction between the educational experience and a marketplace transaction.

2. The student may not, in fact, see the acquisition of knowledge as his real goal. Rather, his purpose may be to acquire a credential or other symbol which will allow him to attain still other ends for which the educational process is simply a means. In this situation conflicts of interest may devel-

4

op, but they are still of a very different order than those existing in the marketplace. Here the student is not asking for something that deprives the instructor of a scarce commodity; rather, the student wishes to be granted a desired outcome, such as a degree, in the least painful and tension-producing manner. In such a situation we have a conflict of goals or of institutionalized means rather than competition for a scarce resource. Furthermore, in such an instance participation in the learning process may be deemed undesirable and in this way quite different from valued goods or services. For these reasons, among others, the analogy that is sometimes drawn between the position of the student and membership in an impaired status group is rather misleading. In most impaired status groups (e.g., an oppressed ethnic minority) there is deprivation of the membership in terms of scarce resources (e.g., goods and services). As I've tried to indicate, this is not characteristic of the student's educational experience.

The above comments are not intended as a denial of the fact that there are some areas of genuine conflict between teachers and students. For example, the teacher may wish to draw his paycheck and attain the highest possible position in his field with a minimum of effort or with his effort directed toward goals which are not compatible with those defined by the student as central (e.g., research). The student, on the other hand, may in fact wish the best possible education (which he may define basically in terms of the overt character of the instructional-learning situation). This may demand an intense commitment in time and devoted study from the instructor. Another example of a potential clash is when an instructor may feel the need to appear as infallible in his judgments. This, in turn, only works against the interest of a student who may have been penalized by what was in fact a very fallible decision. Conflict of interest may also occur *between students* (for a scarce resource) in regard to admission for a fixed number of places in a university or for a grade when the evaluation is done on a "curve." In other words, there are potential clashes of interest which do require careful and explicit protection, but this is not by any means the same as arguing that the nature of the educational enterprise is the same as a marketplace transaction. The significance of the argument being presented is that one must look very carefully at the application of principles from the polity and the market to the educational organization.

Specifically, some of the implications of the above points are as follows:

a. The principles of political democracy do not categorically apply to the educational experience. The educational enterprise contains at least some elements of the socialization process. Furthermore, the "protection" of a political democracy is not required in the same measure as when there is competition for scarce resources. There is no inherent reason why every subsystem needs to be organized along the same lines as the total system. There would be no question, I believe, that the family with young children cannot function as a po-

5

litical entity in the same sense as the nation. This example is not intended to imply that students are equivalent to young children, but it does suggest that there is no immediate reason to draw an analogy from one sector of society to another in all instances. At the same time, enough potential areas of possible conflict have been noted to make it clear that the student should not be expected to rely on the "benevolence" of faculty and administrators or trust in informal primary group processes to insure protection for his legitimate interests when they do clash with those of instructors and other educational personnel.

b. The fact that the educational experience may, in a fundamental sense, be painful and undesired except as a means to quite a different goal suggests that the notion of a predominant consumer preference system in arriving at decisions as to content, modes of evaluation, etc. might well lead to a distortion of the educational experience.[1]

c. I believe that we are in the midst of a general—and, in my opinion, desirable—move from a reliance on traditional authority in society to an emphasis on rational authority. It must be noted, however, that the exercise of rational authority is not automatically equatable with participatory democracy. As a matter of fact, participatory democracy in some areas might be the antithesis of rationality. Also, in the transition from traditional to rational authority one can expect to find outbreaks of irrationality. Approval of the trend toward rational authority does not require, however, acquiescence in irrationality.

3. As long as a group of functionaries are thought to have more knowledge about a subject than the persons they instruct, then to that extent there is a structural inequality that cannot be denied by terms, such as co-learner. This does not in any way deny the fact that both parties may learn from the educational experience and that the nature of the interaction might be one of joint inquiry and discovery. Nevertheless, to pretend that the relationship is totally reciprocal and equal seems, to me, to be a seriously destructive form of self-deception and romanticism. As has already been indicated, such a structural inequality may well be based on rational grounds. It implies that there is a differential competence between the student and the instructor as to at least some aspects of the content which is the subject of the educational experience. This inequality is reinforced in professional education insofar as it is very difficult for the student to know what will prove valuable to him in his practice in the future. It is true, of course, that the instructor, by relying on *past* experiences, may also be in error as to what the demands of the future might be. Nevertheless,

---

[1]It is sometimes argued that the desire for learning in the pure sense is inherent in human beings and it is only a distorting society and formal educational system that smothers such motivation. I would agree with this only in part. Learning difficult material is "painful" and may well be avoided by some even in a much more progressive society.

there is more of a basis to assume that the instructor, if he is familiar with professional practice, may at least have some additional knowledge that would prove useful in making judgments as to necessary content and skills. Also, in professional education the educational organization has a responsibility to the potential recipient of service. This requires that when the student graduates he shall be reasonably competent as a provider of such services. This again is an example of a sharp distinction between the educational enterprise and a marketplace transaction since in the latter situation the interested parties are directly confronting one another without a third party being a major source of concern or responsibility (except in the general sense as society as a whole is an interested party; this also would apply to educational activity).

The second central theme is that of the potential "educational" contribution of students to the governance process. In the previous discussion the distinction was made between interests and competence, as well as between types of interests. The contention that students are not "equal" in relation to making competent decisions in respect to some areas of the educational experience does not imply that they lack all kinds of competence, or that they are unequal in all spheres. As a consumer the student does bring a special and invaluable contribution to the decision-making process. In addition, the student has every right to represent his legitimate interests and to make sure they are fully explicated and understood. Furthermore, because the student's life experience has often been different than that of his teachers, he brings certain insights and understandings that are not likely to be forthcoming from other constituencies in the governance organization. Finally, the very absence of certain responsibilities and commitments allows the student to perceive matters from a different (and important) social perspective. For all these reasons the participation of students in the decision-making process in a regularized and meaningful way is a matter of the greatest *educational* importance. It is particularly crucial that the student not only have a sense of important involvement but that the reality in fact be this.

A third central issue in governance is whether the various constituencies should function primarily as members of joint bodies or whether they should organize along separate constituency lines, with occasional meetings at which time final decision-making will occur. Of course, the two systems are not mutually exclusive and there can be a blending of them in any specific organization. However, it does appear important for the structure of governance to accurately reflect its dynamics.[2] Thus, the pattern of inviting students to be voting members at *faculty* meetings would seem to raise a question as to whether those meetings should in fact be *considered*

---

[2]Once again it needs to be noted that university rules may, in given circumstances, discourage or prohibit "appropriate" structures. The possibility of such constraints should be kept in mind, as a reservation, throughout the ensuing discussion.

faculty meetings. It might be more desirable to have the faculty hold its own meetings periodically to discuss matters of mutual concern and to have the same thing done by the students and civil service employees. Then, however, *decision-making* for the school could take place at a meeting that might be referred to as the *school* senate (rather than conceiving of the *decision-making* forum as being the *faculty* meeting). There is the implication in my comments that civil service personnel also have an interest that may need representation in the governance structure. Of course, there is nothing in the "constituency" structure that precludes the widest use of joint committees, if that is deemed desirable.[3] Furthermore, the suggested organizational form does not necessarily imply, in any way, "equal" representation in the governing process.

It seems to me that the logic of the preceding discussion provides guidelines in regard to the matter of the extent of representation (including what is sometimes referred to as the "numbers games"). I would contend that on most issues connected with the substance of the educational experience students should not have equal representation in the decision-making process. I base this conclusion on the importance of special knowledge and competence in this kind of policy making. On the other hand, I believe that the students should have sufficient representation, with full voting power, so that they have a sense of reasonable security and confidence in dealing with the larger and sometimes "psychologically coercive" faculty. As long as the principle is recognized that the importance and right to representation does not automatically imply equal weight, then it would seem to me that most committees, including those dealing with personnel matters, should have students as full participants. On some committees, though, students will have to act as individuals, rather than as representatives of a constituency, in order to maintain confidentiality.

A fourth major concern, that of the centralization of power, and the related issue of the diffusion of authority have come to occupy a front and center position in recent years. In this respect I would like to point out that the extreme diffusion of authority can sometimes have the unanticipated consequence of actually centralizing decision-making powers, through informal channels, because of the hiatus of such institutionalized power at middle levels. An opposite consequence which is sometimes encountered is that of the immobilization of a given unit because of the absence of effective decision-makers. It should also be recognized that the delegation of authority and power presupposes that there is a person or unit to whom such delegation can be made in an effective and accountable manner.

A fifth area of importance concerns the matter of "due process" and re-

---

[3] I will not, in this paper, explore the nature of the concept of "cooptation." However, for the purposes at hand I am making the assumption that cooperation between the various constituencies, including work on committees and other bodies, does not necessarily lead to the emasculation of a reform movement nor to the betrayal of student interests.

ated procedures. One sometimes hears experienced teachers expressing concern about the formalization of procedures, such as those dealing with grievances. The basis for such doubt is not usually a desire to perpetuate inequities but rather the belief that the relationships between students and teachers should be based on mutual good will and trust, with supporting norms. It is sometimes argued that positive relationships between the various parties are likely to be impaired by formalized procedures which may prove, in the long run, even less effective in guaranteeing the rights of the respective parties than an appropriate normative structure. Although I have a certain sympathy for this position and recognize how important it is for procedures to have a supporting normative system if they are to be effective over a period of time, I would still maintain the position that adequate protection for the various constituencies does require formalized procedures. A reliance on benevolence or on the pretense that no potential conflicts of interest exist may, in fact, result in serious injury to the legitimate rights of any or all of the constituencies. Of course, an over reliance on complex procedures, or on form rather than substance, can lead to rigidity and inequity. But this is not a necessary consequence of instituting adequate formalized procedures.

Finally, an intra-faculty issue that often arises has to do with the role of non-tenured or junior faculty members in personnel decisions. It is frequently argued that the vested interests (e.g., mobility aspirations) of junior faculty prevent them from making an objective assessment of colleagues at similar levels when matter of tenure or promotion are being considered. The reason, of course, is that they are presumably competing with one another for the same thing; thus they are said to react at poles—either too gently or extremely harsh. On the other hand, it should be noted that senior faculty also have certain interests that are frequently apparent, such as the replication of self or one's own program. It seems to me that participation by all levels in such matters is important and desirable.

The present monograph is not designed as a book of solutions or as a blueprint of governance structures. I believe, however, that the reader will find it stimulating and that perhaps it may assist in the development of more effective patterns for governance arrangements.

Herbert Bisno, Dean,
Raymond A. Kent School of Social Work,
University of Louisville,
and Chairman,
CSWE Committee on Students

9

CONTRIBUTING AUTHORS*

Winifred Bell, Professor, School of Social Work, State University of New York at Albany

Kingman Brewster, Jr., President, Yale University

Charles Frankel, Professor, Department of Philosophy, Columbia University

Phyllis Caroff, Assistant Professor, School of Social Work, Hunter College of the City University of New York

D. Bruce Johnstone, Assistant Director, Center for Economic Education, University of Minnesota

Fred N. Kerlinger, Professor, Educational Psychology, New York University

Lillian C. Lampkin, Professor, School of Social Work, Hunter College of the City University of New York

Earl J. McGrath, Director, Center of Higher Education, Temple University

Frank J. Peirce, Associate Dean, School of Social Professions, University of Kentucky

Lilian Ripple, Associate Executive Director, Council on Social Work Education

Paul Schreiber, Dean, School of Social Work, Hunter College of the City University of New York

Jay C. Shaffer, Student, Law School, Harvard University

Carl Slater, Fellow, Center for the Study of Medical Education, University of Illinois College of Medicine

Patricia J. Stickney, Consultant on Students, Council on Social Work Education

Edward Allan Swanson, Student, School of Social Work, University of Washington

Joseph Vigilante, Dean, School of Social Work, Adelphi University

---

*Affiliations given were those at the time the articles included in this volume were written.

GENERAL ISSUES
REGARDING STUDENT
RIGHTS AND RESPONSIBILITIES

STUDENTS' RIGHTS AND RESPONSIBILITIES IN GRADUATE SCHOOLS OF SOCIAL WORK: SURVEY OF CURRENT PRACTICE

LILIAN RIPPLE

N PREPARATION FOR DISCUSSION at a meeting of deans and direc-
rs of graduate schools of social work in January, 1969, CSWE conducted
 quick and fairly superficial inquiry in October, 1968. Its purpose was
 obtain a somewhat better indication of practices and problems regard-
g students' rights and responsibilities than we might otherwise have. In
1e usual course of events, information is most readily available on the
ramatic situations that receive a good deal of publicity; in addition,
'SWE is likely to be called upon both by administration and by students
hen difficulties or conflicts arise in individual situations. Obviously, these
urces of information can lead to a distorted view of practice and of prob-
ms.

Before presenting the findings, a word of caution is in order. The findings
fer to the schools' reported practices as of October-November, 1968. In a
tuation that is changing fairly rapidly, by the time data are reported they
re no longer exact. The specific figures used in order to describe the sit-
ation should, therefore, be taken as approximate. The data reported refer
 the 72 accredited schools as of October, 1968.

The questionnaire asked for information on four topics: student partic-
ation in policy development; review of performance when the student's
cademic standing or continuance in school is in question; handling com-
laints or grievances of students; and release of information to prospective
mployers, financing organizations, and others. Classification of responses
 all four of these areas involves some neat problems. On the one hand,
lassification can proceed in terms of degree of explicitness, or formality.
n the other hand, classification can attempt to deal with the substance
f the policy or procedure, regardless of its explicit or formal nature. To

Reprinted from the Social Work Education Reporter, *Vol. 17, No. 2 (June, 1969),*
p. 48-50.

illustrate; a written release by the student to the school to supply reference is a more formal procedure than the decision by the school when, o whether, to provide reference material on request. On the other hand, standard summary to be used for all references, which is seen by the stu dent prior to his graduation, provides a more formal basis for agreemer between student and school than individual response by the school to eac reference request. The two types of formality or explicitness do not neces sarily go together.

STUDENT PARTICIPATION IN POLICY DEVELOPMENT

Three major groupings were found in terms of administrative structure (1) activity is through the student organization; (2) there is a single, over all joint student-faculty committee; and (3) students are members of one o more faculty committees. The differences in terms of administrative struc ture do not wholly represent a hierarchy in terms of real student participa tion.

In 14 schools, student activity related to policy development was throug the student organization. Eight schools reported limited or sporadic activ ity, in spite of some pushing and prodding by deans to get the students t be more active. The situation was very different in the other six school: There was active student involvement which took the form of studer association committees parallel to faculty committees with provision for ex change of ideas, a dean's council, or both.

The second type of participation was through a joint student-facult liaison committee, also found in 14 schools. At the time the questionnaire were returned, about half of these schools were considering other forms c committee involvement of students. In all 14 schools the student member of the joint committee were elected by the student body or appointed b the student association. The faculty members generally were appointe by the dean but, in two or three schools, were elected. Students consti tuted 30 to 40 percent of the committee membership at five schools, one half at five schools, and two-thirds at three schools (one school not reportin size.)

The majority of schools had student members on one or more facult committees. In almost half of these 44 schools there was a written agree ment or guide regarding student members; the 20 with such written state ments do not appear to differ in the extent and type of student participatio from the 24 whose organizational structure was based upon "general un derstanding." The number of committees on which students had member ship varied greatly, primarily associated with the committee structure in th school. In a few schools, students were members of only one or two com mittees, usually including the curriculum committee. In general, howeve students were members of all committees with the exception of those cor

14

erned with faculty appointments, tenure, etc., and to a lesser extent, those concerned with review of student performance.

Students were participating but non-voting members of committees in 3 schools. A number of these noted that official voting was not permitted by university regulations; most schools commented that voting as such was relatively unimportant since decisions generally were arrived at by concensus. Most commonly, there were two or three student members on a committee and students constituted 25 to 40 percent of the membership. Only eight schools reported any committee with only one student member and this was customary at only two of the 44 schools. Conversely, ten schools reported four or more students on at least some committees.

There are some differences in type of student participation by size of school. Of the 27 schools with full-time enrollment of less than 125, almost half (13 schools) had student members on faculty committees, and the remainder were evenly divided between the other two types of participation —student-faculty committees and activity through the student association. There was no further differentiation by size of school; the medium and large schools had just about the same proportions with the several types of participation, a little more than 60 percent with participation on faculty committees.

Schools were also asked about any problems encountered "in acquiring students for committee membership, or other form of involvement, or in achieving meaningful participation on their part." As the extent of provision for participation increased, so too did the number of schools reporting problems. Omitting the eight schools with minimal, if any, activity through the student association, there are three main groups. In the 20 schools with active participation through the student association or with student-faculty committees, 15 reported no problems; in the 13 schools with non-voting student participation on committees, nine reported no problems; among the 31 schools with voting members on faculty committees, 11 reported no problems. Or, to put it another way, the proportion reporting problems was 25 percent, 30 percent, and 65 percent. The greater extent of problems reported by this last group relates, apparently, to two factors. First, this represents the most extensive and intensive participation which inevitably brings with it problems that need to be solved. Second, and perhaps more important, voting committee membership is the last stage in a developing plan of participation. These schools were beginning to experience the "letdown" or waning of interest that occurs when committee work begins to pile up and becomes an onerous burden rather than a stimulating opportunity.

The problems reported were of three types and, interestingly, schools that noted any problems tended to deal with one primary problem. In all, to recapitulate, there were 29 reports of problems from 64 schools (omits the eight with limited student organization activity). Twelve concerned time,

15

eight concerned representativeness of student members, and nine concerned quality of participation. Problems with time cover two situations: the actual amount of time required for participation which reduces the student's time for his educational program and "timing" which necessitates having meetings at very difficult hours (early morning or evening) if students are not to miss class or field work. The "representativeness" problem concerns the fact that students who participate are volunteers in one way or another and that whether they represent the student body or their own views is often difficult to establish. The problem of quality of participation, in particular, appears to develop as time goes on; several responses referred to differences this year compared with last year or the year before. Once student membership on committees has been established and accepted, attendance tends to become sporadic, particularly in duller committees, and preparation for a meeting is scanty or lacking. Students apparently behave no differently than the rest of us.

PROCEDURES FOR HANDLING GRIEVANCES

With the exception of procedures for handling matters relating to review of student performance, most schools do not have specific procedures for handling individual or group grievances. Typically, the student may appeal to the faculty advisor or any member of the faculty, including the dean on specific issues. Whether complaints involving more than one student are channeled through the student organization, a student-faculty committee, specific faculty committees on which students are represented, or some other form of making representations to the faculty or dean depends upon the type of school organization.

REVIEW OF STUDENT PERFORMANCE

Schools were asked to report what procedures they have for review of performance when the student's academic standing or continuance in school is in question. The responses indicate three basic patterns: (1) 21 schools did not have formal established procedures; (2) 25 schools reported a formal established procedure but submitted no written material and the information suggested an "understood" method without written formalization; and (3) 25 schools had formal established procedures guided by a written document (one school did not respond).

Regardless of the degree of formality, there are three main approaches to review of student performance. First is a very informal approach that involves considerable work with the faculty advisor who may utilize other faculty or the dean in making crucial decisions. This procedure characterized 13 schools, with the student having appeal machinery available in two of them. As might be expected, this method we found in only one of the 25

16

schools with formalized written procedures and was most common among the 21 schools with no formalized procedures.

The second pattern involves use of the entire faculty in reviewing situations of problematic academic performance. Eight of the ten schools utilizing this method were in the group with no written formalized procedures.

The third, and most common, method is to use a committee: in 16 schools an *ad hoc* committee was set up for each student review situation although there might be one or two regular members, such as the dean or associate dean, director of field work, or director of admissions. In 32 schools there was a standing committee which might be augmented by the particular student's faculty advisor and current instructors. There are undoubtedly some psychological differences in these two types of committees, but they appear to operate essentially in the same way. Combining the two types of committees, we find that provision was made for the student to present material to the committee in 16 of these 48 schools. Most commonly, the provision was for the student to be notified of the meeting and invited to submit material or to appear in person to discuss his situation. In five of these schools the student could bring an "advocate" with him who, in some instances, had to be a member of the current student body. In eight of these 16 schools plus three others, or a total of 11, a formal procedure for appeal from the committee's decision was provided.

The committees to review student performance, whether *ad hoc* or standing, were generally composed of faculty members appointed by the dean. Five schools reported student members on the committees that review the performance of other students; one school reported student members who, however, were excluded when confidential material regarding the problems of particular students was being discussed.

The provision made for review of student performance is related to size of school. Review committees were reported by 83 percent of the large schools, 73 percent of the medium-sized schools, and 52 percent of the small schools. Only one of the large schools relied primarily upon the faculty advisors, and use of the entire faculty was largely a practice in the smaller schools.

RELEASE OF INFORMATION ABOUT STUDENTS

Schools were asked to describe their basic policy regarding release of information about students to prospective employers, organizations providing financial aid, investigative agencies, and other inquirers. They were, further, asked to note whether they differentiated between academic and other types of information. Conditions under which information is released and the type of information supplied vary greatly. With respect to prospective employers, one may presume that the student, or former student, has con-

17

sented to the release of information since he has requested that a reference be sent. Twenty schools reported a more specific form of consent: 11 schools use a standard summary which the student sees and nine schools require a signed "release of information." In five of the latter, however, the student signs a release but does not see the letter or report that is sent. The majority of schools, even though not requiring a signed release or using a standard summary which the student sees, stressed that their reference letters deal with performance and not with process, progress, or personality assessment. On the other hand, a small group (13 schools) noted the contrary: they supply educational assessments and rather full information about strengths, weaknesses, personality, and adjustment.

There is no particular relationship between type and extent of information released to prospective employers and size of school. The smaller schools tended to be at both extremes, constituting half of the schools that used a standard summary which was seen by the student and, also, half of those that released considerable evaluative material.

Policy on reports to organizations providing financial aid generally was similar to the school's policy regarding reports to prospective employers. Variations were in the direction of supplying less information, usually on the basis that reports made while the student's education was still in process were highly tentative and might be misunderstood by the financing organization. This was the only area mentioned as one presenting problems. Where the student is on leave from an agency that is financing his education, some schools have had difficulty in trying to limit the information supplied.

Responses regarding handling inquiries for information from other sources were meager. In spite of specific mention in the questionnaire of governmental investigative bureaus, over half the schools made no response to this question. With such a high non-respondent rate, the answers obtained are meaningless. All that can be said for certain is that six schools reported that they supply no information and 17 reported that they release basic objective data only, usually that the person is or was a student and the degree awarded.

SUMMARY

The inquiry covered two quite distinct aspects of students' rights and responsibilities: first, their participation in development of policy and, second, the procedures to safeguard assessment of their performance and the release of information regarding them. Formal means for student participation, especially on faculty committees, is quite new in most schools and has come as a response to a changing climate on university campuses. Currently, the trend is clearly in this direction with problems for the future primarily centering around the age-old ones of achieving and maintaining effective committee involvement. Procedures to safeguard students' rights and interests are of much longer standing and were initiated by faculties over the years. There appears to be little relationship between the two types of policies or procedures. That is, a school with explicit formal procedures for student participation in policy development is not more likely to have explicit formal procedure for review of student performance or release of information than a school where participation in policy development is more informal. Put another way, when all three aspects are examined together, only three schools reported explicit formal procedures in each while another nine were close to across-the-board explication, formality, and protection. At the other extreme, the most informal or unstructured approach in all three areas was true for no school.

In conclusion, the findings of this brief survey show that considerable change has taken place in the policies and practices of graduate schools with respect to students' rights and responsibilities. There is much unevenness and, already, further changes are in process as experience is gained with new patterns. The most immediate need appears to be the development of viable methods of implementation.

SOME ISSUES IDENTIFIED BY THE GRADUATE SCHOOLS OF SOCIAL WORK REGARDING STUDENT RIGHTS AND RESPONSIBILITIES

PATRICIA J. STICKNEY

THIS PAPER IS AN ATTEMPT to highlight certain themes and issues on student rights and responsibilities as reported by graduate schools during 1968-69. It supplements the papers prepared by Lilian Ripple and Gordon Hearn for the January, 1969 Deans and Directors Meeting in Cleveland. In preparing this working paper, I have borrowed liberally from the communications of deans and various individuals in graduate education for social work. Unfortunately I have not had readily available material from the students themselves, as CSWE queries were always directed to the schools and not through student channels. I hope the paper will serve as a stimulus to the discussion and development of general positions and recommended approaches to student rights and responsibilities.

GENERAL ISSUES AND TRENDS

Student unrest in graduate professional schools has been on the increase within the last couple of years. Students, faculty, administrators—all are searching for a definition of their responsibilities and their rights. The students want a more influential role in the educational process with participation in decision making.

As one dean noted, the viability of schools depends upon student participation in and contributions to the life and quality of the institutions. In recent years in the universities there is a sharpened focus on student-institution relationships. The national issues that led to student unrest in the past—Vietnam, the draft, and racial oppression—are still present in the

Reprinted from the Social Work Education Reporter, *Vol. 18, No. 1 (March, 1970), pp. 25-27, 64.*

ninds of students, but for many students, the immediate concerns have be-
ome reform in educational practices and the extent to which the universi-
ies are responsive to the people living nearby. In the graduate and profes-
ional schools, particularly, many of the student demands are changing
rom attacks on the institutions and their administrative set-ups—par-
icularly as related to national policy and the larger community—to criticism
f the curriculum and the students' recognition of their stake in the educa-
ional program and their future professional life. Greater emphasis seems to
e being placed on the quality of education and equality of opportunity in
ducation.

One dean emphasized that for the majority of students what really mat-
ers is the quality of the relationships between students and faculty. This de-
ends not on contractual papers but on mutual give and take in a dynamic
elationship. Given real confidence and adequate communication, this dean
elt that policies and procedures were only a means to the end of collabora-
ion—with the formal arrangements changing and evolving all the time to
neet the needs of the partners.

The overwhelming majority of the schools of social work reported in
all, 1968, and again in spring, 1969, that they were in the process of devel-
ping and/or revising their policies and procedures regarding student rights
nd responsibilities. Among the many reasons for these developments in
chools of social work was the drafting in 1967 of the Joint Statement on
Rights and Freedom of Students by representatives from the American
Association of University Professors, U.S. National Student Association,
Association of American Colleges, National Association of Student Personnel Administrators, and National Association of Women Deans and Counselors. This Joint Statement was adopted by the CSWE Board of Directors
in November, 1968 and by many colleges, universities, and educational associations throughout the country. In addition to the promotion of acceptance of these new standards on an institutional level, there have been joint
approaches to regional accrediting agencies to seek embodiment of the new
principles in standards for accreditation. For example, the new accreditation standard on student rights for graduate professional schools of social
work calls attention to the need for a school to have "procedures to protect
students against prejudiced or capricious academic evaluations, improper
disclosure of student views, beliefs, and political associations, and limitations upon freedom of expression." Also, schools will need to have procedures to "guarantee the students the right to organize in their own interests
as students," so that "students can contribute to the formulation of institutional policy affecting academic and student affairs."

Graduate schools of social work, in reply to the CSWE queries in 1968-
69, highlighted a number of issues to be considered before developing any
general position or stance regarding: (1) student participation in policy
development; (2) review of student performance; (3) handling of complaints

or grievances of students; and (4) student records and release of information about students.

STUDENT PARTICIPATION IN POLICY DEVELOPMENT

There are many reasons why schools are seeking student involvement in policy development. There is a common belief that students should have an opportunity to take part in the shaping and directions of the programs, activities, and regulations which affect them, their education, and their future professional life. For many, the education of the student is enhanced by such participation in the decision-making process of the institution in which he is part. As one educator noted, participating in vital decisions improves morale, productivity, and quality of work.

Schools are moving toward arrangements for students to participate more visibly and formally in the making of educational decisions. Many schools want a dialogue between faculty and students through which the experiences and ideas of all can contribute to the continuing development of education for the profession. As one school noted, such student-faculty dialogue in joint committees unfolds a more realistic picture of curriculum problems than is possible with isolated and insulated groups of students and faculty working separately. An administrator commented that the movement toward student participation is not based so much on rights as upon considerations of good educational and administrative practice.

Schools, in reporting their experiences, indicated that considerations of student participation have been made in the context that faculty have the final authority for educational policy and that the dean, in turn to the provost and president, is responsible for the organization, fiscal management, and personnel.

In order to have meaningful student involvement, there must be: effective communications; representation of informed opinion from faculty and students; a dialogue on matters of policy between persons who are qualified by experience, information, and effective contact with their varying constituencies; and a formulation and articulation of the educational program and its goals. Schools have noted that the failure or lack of any of these aforementioned elements will result in campus unrest.

Schools are trying to determine when, where, and to what extent students' participation in policy development will detract from the educational experience. Different models for student involvement are being tested, such as (1) collaboration with student representatives integrated into regular structure; (2) a bicameral form of school government with faculty and student legislative houses and with joint standing committees; or (3) joint student-faculty committees or increased faculty time for individual conferences or a combination of these or other methods.

Student involvement in academic affairs challenges professors in their areas of competence. How and to what degree should the student voice be eard in curriculum development? At the extremes of faculty opinion are those against any student voice and those for total abdication to student demands. What part should students play in determining the relevance and value of different uses of their time? What are mutual and common concerns of faculty and students and what are the differences in role and accountability? Schools reported lack of understanding due to the varying perceptions of appropriate roles and responsibilities of students and faculty.

There are other subtle general issues regarding participation of students in policy decision making. Students are imaginative but inexperienced. They are only in school for two years and on committees for only a shorter period. It takes time on most committees for new members to learn enough to become genuinely useful. Furthermore, student styles and opinions often change quickly. Within two years students graduate, but the administration and faculty are left with the policies they helped devise. Oftentimes students feel an urgency for change, as they bring a different and shortened perspective into the consideration of matters of policy. In graduate professional schools particularly, a continuity of perspective and some sense of the time dimension are essential.

Some schools reported that there are frequently outside pressures against student participation from such sources as legislators, regents, and other school administrators. One school reported as a major problem the students' political attitude toward the educational process and structure.

Problems concerning the acquiring of student participants were reported. Questions have been raised whether students should be elected or appointed by the entire student body or through the student associations. Selection of students for participation by students does not necessarily produce students best-suited to contribute to the education of other students or to the committee. Faculty appointment of students, however, negates the right of students to name representatives and to require accountability to students. Two administrators agreed that specific students should be selected to serve on specific committees. Schools reported that they had an inadequate representation of the range of student opinion and ideas in the conduct of their schools. The need for greater participation of ethnic minority students was noted. Schools are trying to find the best means for securing competence, interest, and representativeness for student membership. One school commented that too often the student participants are volunteers and include only a very small minority of the total student body.

Whether students represent their own views or those of other students is often difficult to establish. Some schools noted that if students are selected through an election process there is greater realization of their representative functions. Frequently, there are problems around the nature and extent of student feedback. Effective ways for students to communicate the deliberations, directions, and decisions need to be developed.

Another problem area relates to the time and "timing" of student participation. The actual amount of time required for participation reduces the student's time for his educational program. Question was raised as to how many meetings a student can attend without affecting his class and field work. Also there are problems around scheduling of meetings so students can attend. Often, meetings are scheduled at the convenience of faculty rather than consideration of when students can attend without conflict to class or field work. Schools with block field placements have different problems in scheduling meetings. Delays are experienced concerning the length of time it may take the student body to get connected with an issue. The incoming first-year class requires a period of time to elect representatives. This often results in delays in the initial stage of the committee process.

Problems around the quality of student participation appear to develop as time goes on. In the beginning, problems in achieving full student participation develop because of the need to devote committee time to educating the student to committee membership or committee work. Later on for some schools it became a problem of how to achieve meaningful, sustained involvement of students in policy development with students' apathetic attitude toward some committee work or short interest in some activities, particularly with increasing demands of their own educational program on their time. Some schools report declining student interest at the prospect of additional labor and time needed for full participation. With lags in student interest, the problems then develop around continuity of student participation.

Another set of issues concerns how to structure student participation. Should the participation be through the student organization, joint student-faculty committees, some or all faculty committees, an open door policy for administrators, a combination of these, or some other method? Should students serve on all committees or should they be excluded from some, such as those mentioned most frequently—for example: committees concerned with faculty appointments, tenure, promotions, and those concerned with review of individual student performance. One school reported that not all school committees that wanted student participation have it, because students are not interested in some committees and feel they do not have much to contribute. Therefore, under these circumstances encouraging student participation may become a kind of tokenism. Should students have equal representation on all committees or different representation on different committees? Should field work time and credit be given for student participation in committee work? Schools commented that since committee decisions were arrived at by consensus, the fact that students are voting or non-voting members was unimportant and caused no special problems.

Schools reported a number of alternative ways for student participation in policy development. In addition to the aforementioned ways of student involvement and student input, the following were mentioned: faculty-stu-

24

nt retreats; student run weekly faculty-student colloquims; noon-time
eetings and informal luncheons; increased faculty time for individual stu-
nt conferences; questionnaires and/or other forms of student evaluation
classes, field work and educational program; informal seminars at fac-
ty homes; student orientation committees to plan and conduct orientation
rograms; student curriculum committees; end of year, day long public
aring for all students to testify on changes desired in curriculum and in
hool; regular meetings of dean and students; all day discussions of gen-
al problems, held on a regular basis for students, faculty members, and
dministrators; student responsibilities for extra-curricular guest lec-
res; university committee on personnel interviewing selected students re-
arding faculty tenure, promotion and contract; parallel student commit-
es with mechanisms for recommending policy; and student-planned and
d courses.

EVIEW OF STUDENT PERFORMANCE

chools raised a number of questions and issues about the current practices
nd procedures for review of student performance. Should all students be
eriodically reviewed or just students who are having educational prob-
ms? Is a student having academic problems best served by an *ad hoc* stu-
ent review committee, by a constituted committee that has experience, by
he entire faculty or some other method? Schools commented that their
cademic grievance procedures should insure due process for the student,
ight of appeal, and right of counsel if the student desires it.

A problem develops when students think of the student review proce-
ures as a part of a disciplinary process rather than a review of the educa-
ional assessment. Sometimes, students feel that with a formal set of re-
iew procedures they have to "play the game" by "confessing their sins."

Schools recognize their right and responsibilities to attest to persons'
itness to practice social work. However, faculty frequently have not come
o grips with the need to have student performance reflected in grades.
There are psychological problems in grading, with frequent variability
mong faculty, which results in inequities in grading. It has been noted that
rades for class work can be fairly objective, but for field work there is
reater chance of subjectivity. Schools recognize the need to be clearer
bout what competent professional practice is and to develop appropriate
ndices to more objectively assess field work performance.

HANDLING OF GRIEVANCES OR COMPLAINTS BY STUDENTS

Although most schools do not have specific procedures for handling individual or group grievances, most schools encourage the student to appeal
o the faculty advisor or member of faculty, including the dean on specific

issues. When complaints involve more than one student, the student organization, a student-faculty committee, or specific faculty committees on which students are represented, are the usual channels for students to express dissatisfactions and get a fair hearing.

One school established a standing grievance committee upon the insistence of the students—only to find that students used other established channels to air their differences. Another school will have a student-faculty ombudsman to study and gather information on the situation presented, to serve as mediator, and, if an agreement cannot be reached, to convene an *ad hoc* committee to make recommendations to the dean.

As one administrator commented, there are few problems if there are open channels of communication for students to state and resolve grievances and if there is a genuine, creative partnership between faculty and students.

STUDENT RECORDS AND RELEASE OF INFORMATION ABOUT STUDENTS

With the increasing concern for the protection of civil rights, educational institutions are reassessing the whole question as to: what information about students should be sought and from what sources and for what reason; where, and how and how long should information be kept; who should have access to it; how the student should be involved in the process; what are the student rights and what are the institution's responsibilities. In order to safeguard civil rights, schools are finding an increasing need to formalize and make known their policies and procedures in this area. Also with the new accreditation standard, schools should have "procedures to protect students against improper disclosure of student views, beliefs, and political associations." The Joint Statement on Rights and Freedoms of Students, in dealing with the student records, states that "institutions should have a carefully considered policy as to the information which should be part of a student's permanent educational record and as to the conditions of its disclosure," and then details other provisions necessary in the gathering, maintenance, and disclosure of student records.

In the survey of the schools, the conditions under which information is released and the type of information supplied vary greatly. The majority of schools, although not requiring a signed release or using a standard summary which the student sees, stressed that reference letters deal with performance and not with process, progress, or personality assessment.

Very few problems were cited by the schools in this area. Schools appear to have some trouble in determining the kind and amount of information about students that is appropriate to supply to: (1) employers who are sending employees to school with full pay under a work-study plan; (2) organizations providing student financial aid—with or without a work commit-nent; and (3) prospective employers. For example, schools have had diffiulty in defining the limits of the information to be supplied to these social work colleagues.

Other issues that were alluded to but not resolved were: whether a student should know what is in his student folder and in the official reference; whether a student should determine to whom information is given; how much and what kind of information should be released; problems of obsolete information and need for periodic review of data and destruction of materials; frequent requests of lists of students for research purposes and or membership organizations; special problems regarding requests for information about applicants or about students prior to matriculation; telephone requests for information; conflict of rights of privacy; and right of government to ask information.

With the current methods of data processing, microfilming of records, and data retrieval, the problems regarding release of student information have multiplied. In the light of this and in order to protect the students' rights of privacy, schools will want to reassess their procedures for the gathering, storing, retrieving, and giving of information on students.

FUTURE DIRECTIONS

From the information gathered from schools of social work this past year, we can only speculate on some of the reasons for student unrest and student dissatisfactions with social work education. There appears to be pervasive dissatisfactions with the educational experience which no attention to structure alone will correct. These dissatisfactions are at times focused on the curriculum or on the quality and methods of teaching. Sometimes there are dissatisfactions with the milieu of the school, where the quality of executive leadership leaves something to be desired. Another major area of student dissatisfaction centers around ethnic minority concerns with increasing demands for more minority students and faculty and a more relevant curriculum.

At this point in the Committee on Students' examination of student rights and responsibilities, it seems to me that we have not defined as yet the nature and scope of student concerns nor where the Committee should focus its attention. With further study and a student input in our deliberations, I know the Committee can contribute to the quality of student life and of student-institution relations in social work education.

STUDENT PARTICIPATION
IN DECISION MAKING
IN SCHOOLS OF SOCIAL WORK

STUDENT INVOLVEMENT
IN ADMINISTRATION
AND POLICY FORMATION
AND IN EDUCATIONAL PROGRAMS
AND CURRICULUM DEVELOPMENT

PAUL SCHREIBER

THE CONTROVERSIAL NATURE of this topic cannot be camouflaged by its bland and formal title; the raw elements of the implied issues and the highly charged overtones of their implementation will rise to the surface and demand the attention which they deserve. While the issue itself—participation by students in the educational process, or, in the language of the lapel button, Student Power—is not new or original, while the tension between the "establishment" of higher education and the student body is as old and, probably, as fundamental and inevitable as the conflict between the generations, of which it is a legitimate part, their appearance and their intensity fluctuate and reflect the societal and cultural—and frequently also the moral—currents and trends of the period. Although the form of student expression might bring discomfort to the university and pain to the representatives of faculty and administration who have to bear the brunt of any confrontation, the underlying issues are perennial. This may disappoint the students, to whom anything or anybody over 30 is slightly suspect—perhaps rightly, since there is relatively little evidence that age automatically improves anything except good wine.

There are several ways to explore this unwieldy topic. One could survey the current scene and obtain from the member schools of the council an overview of prevailing practices, arrangements, and relationship patterns. As a researcher, I was naturally tempted to conduct such a survey. But a certain degree of laziness and a reluctance to impose still another questionnaire on my colleagues—I know how I would have reacted, had I been on the receiving end—led very early to discarding this particular method. I

Reprinted from the Social Work Education Reporter, *Vol. 16, No. 4 (December, 1968), pp. 55-58, 67-68.*

could have systematically picked other people's brains—New York City, with six schools, a variety of other educational institutions, and a number of national and local agencies involved in social work education, is an ideal location for such an undertaking. I gave that up, too, as a major method, although obviously other people's opinions are reflected in what I have to say.

It seems to me that the issues in this topic, because of their pervasive and enduring quality, lend themselves most properly to a rational, sober, and non-belligerent analytical review as the only defensible basis from which one can proceed with an appropriate course of action. That I happen to be a dean is of little consequence in the discussion.

This topic can be neatly divided and subdivided into Administration and Policy Formulation on the one hand, and Educational Program and Curriculum Development on the other. While I propose to follow this format in general, I must warn you that reality is not nearly as tightly compartmentalized and tidy as this, and that considerable overlapping and intermixing occur.

The magic word, of course, is the operating term: Involvement. My pocket Oxford Dictionary mentions under "involve": entangle, implicate (in a charge or crime), imply or entail; and under involvement: especially financial embarrassment. These, however, are not necessarily the meanings we have in mind. Let us assume that, in our discussion, involvement refers to responsible and meaningful participation by students in the enumerated areas and activities.

Historically, precedents can be found for either extreme of an involvement scale if we want to measure the degree of participation. By the second half of the thirteenth century, the medieval student universities were participating, through their elected representatives and their nations, not only in the election of their own rector (president) but also in the general administration and direction of the entire study process.

Carleton University in Ottawa, Canada, represents an interesting modern version of a university with the maximum degree of student involvement. According to information received from Father Bowers, in the coming academic year there will be student representatives on the Senate, on Faculty Boards, and on the Faculty Council of the School of Social Work; they will take part in the deliberations and decisions of departments and other bodies responsible for programs of instruction. Student representation on the Board of Governors has also been agreed to, in principle. Father Bowers notes that these proposals did not really originate with the students, but with a special joint committee of the Senate and the Board of Governors, who recognized that the students wanted and needed to participate in university government. Examples of the other extreme, the completely faculty- and board-regulated university and curriculum, are numerous and, I am sure, familiar.

What we are concerned with, then, is the nature of student participation in the different areas under discussion, its appropriateness and degree. Hopefully, this review will increase the clarity and reduce the heat so often engendered when lines are drawn, and perhaps indicate a few ways in which participation can have the most impact on students and university and, at the same time, achieve the most positive and constructive results.

In emphasizing the impact on the school as a whole, the objectives of student participation are extended beyond a "good learning experience." Viewing it as an exercise that is "good for the student" seems to constitute a rather narrow and somewhat synthetic goal. If the university is to be truly an academic community, then participation must mean that all parts of the school must share in promoting the common enterprise.

Two points remain in this introduction which require clarification: place and time. We are discussing students in a professional school, students who have successfully completed a baccalaureate education and who now want to prepare for a career and later a profession. It is obvious that the prerequisite of a baccalaureate degree introduces a certain age factor, and that, even though our student body has become progressively younger, the overwhelming majority are no longer minors. In the context of the professional or the graduate school, whether the university acts *in loco parentis* is of no concern. This removes, fortunately, one of the issues which often beclouds undergraduate student involvement. For the same reason, the problem of controlling the student's extracurricular life usually does not arise. In this respect, I see no difference between students in graduate and professional schools; but in respect to the objectives of education, there is a fundamental and significant difference between the traditional graduate school and the professional school, and, therefore, between their students. While both share the undergraduate experience, their goals and commitments are very different.

The student in the professional school wants to become a practitioner, a doer, a member of a helping profession. The school, in turn, must assist him in becoming consciously the kind of person who knows, acts, and feels in a way that enables him to help others—individuals, groups, and communities —in need of services, knowledge, attitudes, and skills which they do not have. If this were not so, we would not need organized educational programs to introduce neophytes to the subculture of the profession. Indeed, before professionalization—and perhaps after its introduction, too—anybody and everybody acted upon the assumption that they could help others in need. Only as the necessity of training and, later on, of education was recognized, were practice methodology and a set of ethical values developed to differentiate the qualified practitioner from the lay person. It follows that this has some bearing on the role of the student in the professional school.

Outlining the time context in which we must place this review, while infinitely more complicated, is indispensable if the issues are to be fully understood and appreciated. I realize that I am confronted here with an in-

superable disadvantage, the irremovable actuality of age which, decisivel
and, in the eyes of my students, fatally, prevents full understanding an
appreciation of the vital issues confronting today's students. I mean thi
seriously. The best I can do, under the circumstances, is to try to delineate
the salient conditions bearing upon the issues under review.

It is trite to say that we live in troubled times. And yet the uneasiness an
confusion, "restlessness," as the President in his State of the Union mes
sage called it, which pervade all of us, most significantly affect students an
faculties alike, even including administrators. We have become disillu
sioned with the values and mores of a society, which on the one hand seem
to occupy itself with material gains and senseless hedonism, and on th
other toys with weapons of ultimate destruction and engages in senseles
wars while neglecting domestic inequities and injustices. We are trouble
by the discrepancy between technological progress and societal ineptitude
It is the legitimate privilege of the young to blame their predecessors fo
this sorry state of affairs and logical for them to demand the responsibilit
and the right to change and correct the sins and errors of the past. Olde
experts have proved their impotence and irrelevance; they have gotten u
into this mess and can only perpetuate it. Consequently, the argument goes
the students must be not only involved but powerful; they must be given a
voice in decisions and policies affecting them.

It is difficult to argue rationally against a position conceived in such
simplistic and general terms. But reality is not black and white; it is a complex web of currents and counter-currents, in which each generation, to
establish its own frame of reference, must take into account the past as
well as the future. No revolution starts *de novo* but builds on the precepts
and lessons of the past.

Another serious factor is that today's students have been exposed to a
variety of experiences which have caused them to participate far more fully
in social action during their college years than have students of the past. It
is significant that many of these activities emphasize social and ethical
values, and indicate a sharpened sense of purpose and direction.[1] Out of this
arises one of the most difficult and complex controversies underlying the
struggle for participation and which is reflected throughout the profession.
The proper role of action, the very nature of social work, its limits and its
boundaries, are undergoing searching scrutiny and reevaluation, and the
desire to participate in order to effect change is often a sign of dissatisfaction with the concept of the profession as transmitted by the school.

We would do well to take cognizance of the fundamental issue and
openly discuss it. Stifling the raising of questions may produce disciples,
but will not produce students who are expected to inquire with open minds.
The answers are not in as yet. They will not be found in doctrine or partisan-
ship, but in the passionate and honest, informed and open, search for the

---

[1]Joseph Kate and Nevitt Sandford, "Causes of the Student Revolution," *Saturday Review,*
December 18, 1965, p. 64.

34

ight objectives and values.

Irving Howe raises still another point when he refers to the dependent condition of the graduate student, who is, at the same time, presumed to be serious person, often making notable sacrifices to pursue his studies. Although he speaks of the student in the graduate school, he paints a picture familiar to us in the professional school when he refers to the depressing change in style which the bright and lively undergraduate often undergoes soon after entering graduate school. "He becomes professionally cautious, intellectually timid, concerned to please and adapt to professors. This is hardly a system calculated to encourage manliness and independence of spirit."[2]

Against this background and in the context of these issues we must consider the matter of student involvement. Let me state emphatically that I conceive of "involvement" or "participation" as a system of mutually interdependent rights and responsibilities, obligations, and privileges. There cannot be a one-way street down which participation walks, taking without giving.

My first point, therefore, is an enlargement of the original formulation. Since we are dealing with an institution in which students, faculty, and administration come together for only one purpose, the primary area of involvement has to be the educational process. Only if students, faculty, and administration are all genuinely involved in the educational process can there be fruitful discussion of specific parts of the process. This requires that everyone play an active role, as learner, teacher, and administrator, a prerequisite for effective participation. The student who is not honestly engaged in the learning process is not entitled to be taken seriously; similarly, the teacher who does not meet his primary responsibility of providing optimum instruction and guidance has no right to complain of antagonism and resistance. The administrator must be dedicated to the educational mission of the institution and to the welfare of faculty and students, and willing to take seriously what the university in essence must be: a community of scholars in which each member has a voice that must be not only heard but considered.

Within this overall dimension of positive engagement, what about involvement in administration? Since the term "administration" is rather vague and open to different interpretations, it is difficult to discuss. A quality, however, inherent in administration is that it carries final responsibility and accountability, usually to the president and/or the board of trustees of the university. It is the place where "the buck stops" and cannot be "passed" any further. Corollary to this responsibility must be the right and authority to make a final decision. This does not mean arbitrary or unilateral authoritarianism, but, on the contrary, careful consideration of varying interests and viewpoints, of arguments from all sides, and of various

---

[2]Irving Howe, Introduction, in *Revolution at Berkeley,* M. Miller and S. Gilmore (eds.), (New York: Dial Press, 1965), p. 20.

alternatives. But ultimately the administrator must make his own decision

In the process of clarifying the issues, getting background, and identify ing courses of action and their consequences, it is legitimate for students to present and discuss their point of view, especially if proper recognition is given to all sides of an issue. The students must have the opportunity to pre sent their point of view, listen to the reasons for decisions and policies, and establish communication with the faculty and administration. More than a "hearing" or an outlet for the expression of opinion is needed. If participa tion implies give and take, an open exchange of views and ideas must take place, a frank sharing of reasons and explanations.

Let me use for illustration my own experience at the Hunter College School of Social Work, on which, by necessity, much of my opinion is based. For the past three years I have been meeting monthly in my office with representatives of first- and second-year students, the advisor of the Student Association, and a faculty member. The students prepare an agenda to which we add items when we want to take up certain issues. Min utes are kept by the students and posted in the library. We strive for free and open discussions, dealing with issues rather than complaints, although these cannot always be avoided. We report regularly to the faculty, while the students report to their Association. I believe that this system has been helpful in interpreting and clarifying policy questions; it has provided a forum for the expression of student reaction; it has often resulted in the modification of practices and policies; and it has given to the students a sense of true participation in the affairs of the school. Of particular interest has been the role of the second-year students, who frequently exert a mod erating, much more professionalized influence. I draw attention—parenthet ically—to the difficult problems of representation and representativeness which is troubling the student members of the faculty-student committee and to the related problem of the 50 percent turnover in the constituency, a problem built into any two-year program.

The recent meeting of the Regional Conference of the North-Eastern Schools of Social Work Students in Washington urged that regional and national schools bring all possible pressure to bear on forming faculty-student committees. The committee of students which discussed the matter of student-voting membership on faculty committees modified even the basic consideration of the issue to consider equal, representative faculty-student committees, rather than membership on faculty committees.

A few specific areas within the general framework of administration highlight the problems associated with student involvement. Evaluation of faculty is an administrative responsibility, although in many universities it is shared with a faculty personnel committee. It is unnecessary to elaborate on the generally unsatisfactory state of affairs in regard to methods and criteria of evaluation. It is pertinent, however, to recognize that students have a contribution to make. There is no substitute for their immediate, first-hand experience. Whether students can judge the competence of an in-

36

structor or the validity of the material he presents, they are capable of assessing him as a teacher—and have always done so among themselves—but how can this ongoing informal process be given structure and how can student judgment be used constructively? Many schools and colleges use student surveys, often formulated with the help of faculty members competent in research methodology. Overall findings regarding curriculum, course sequence, and the school's program in general, are then distributed to all students and faculty. But how should the findings concerning the individual instructors of specific courses be handled? Should they be shared with administration and/or with faculty? I do no know whether a satisfactory solution is possible but my own opinion suggests that the students share these findings exclusively with the instructor, who should be trusted to make the fullest use of the results. This does not negate the importance of the administration's awareness of students' reaction to individual instructors. Where there is much smoke, there is usually at least a small fire. But it is equally important that the students' role as a responsible learner be clearly identified and that it be made clear—and insisted upon—that their first responsibility is to bring their reactions to the instructor himself, before any further steps are taken. The good teacher will welcome and respond to this kind of responsible student action and will give it the consideration it deserves. As a teacher, I reject emphatically the argument advanced by a graduate student at last summer's assembly of the National Students' Association. According to a report in the *New York Times,* the young man "noted that he wanted to be a college teacher and 'I don't want to be judged by my intellectual inferiors in my later years.' "

Let me refer, in passing, to a rather sensitive and even more difficult area of faculty evaluation by students. It is implicit in the nature of social work education as clinical education that the student's relationship with his field instructor is usually closer and more intensive than with other members of the classroom faculty, including his faculty advisor. At the same time, he is also more dependent on the field instructor's judgment, in spite of the fact that the instructor frequently is not subject to the direct jurisdiction of the school. Since each field instructor deals with a small number of students, a survey comparable to that of the classroom teacher is not feasible. In this situation, the student's faculty advisor has a key role to play. He must help the advisee to channel his reaction and concern constructively and make sure that they be communicated to field work administration for consideration at the periodical review by school and agency. Many of the recurring difficulties on this matter are undoubtedly related to the very serious problems inherent in the current organization of field instruction.

In many other areas of administration—such as scholarships, schedules, field work procedures, and regulations—the students have a right to be informed not only of rules and criteria, but also of the reasons for them. This implies the right to express their opinions and reactions, and the obligation to consider their opinions carefully. Final decisions, however, would re-

37

main with the administration or, when indicated, with the faculty.

Organizing their own affairs should be the unquestioned prerogative of the students, and they should run and be accountable for their association under the general rules of the school or university. The faculty representative who maintains liaison between the association and the school should be an advisor in the strict sense of the term, leaving initiative and decision to the student body, and intervening only if and when boundaries of legality are openly transgressed. Provisions should be made, through budget and time allocation, to make it possible for the students to carry out this task.

I am not sure that I fully understand what is meant by policy formulation as differentiated from administration. It seems, however, that the same principles apply here, too: responsibility for policy formulation rests with those who are held accountable, either the faculty in regard to educational policy or the administration in regard to administrative policy. One might add that very often final policies in both areas are decided by a higher level than the school itself, and that the school has to operate within and adhere to university-wide policies. It is also important to remember that, in general, the board of trustees of the university is charged, under the charter granted by the state, with ultimate authority for policy.

The scope for student involvement in actual decision-making is, therefore, somewhat limited. Nevertheless, there can and should be ample opportunity for genuine participation in the process of arriving at decisions. Pertinent here is Section IV-C of the Joint Statement on Rights and Freedoms of Students:

> as constituents of the academic community, students should be free, individually and collectively, to express their views on issues of institutional policy and on matters of general interest to the student body.

Turning to the second area of our topic, educational programs and curriculum, it seems relevant to review briefly the role of the student in the professional school. This is a territory into which one steps with justifiable trepidation. No uniform model seems to exist. Much seems to depend on one's basic concept of the nature and function of education. But certain points might be stated. The student comes to school as a learner who wants to be introduced to the profession which he has chosen as a life career. He enters into a contract in which the university is committed to provide him with an appropriate education, with goals sanctioned by the profession and the academic community. The student, in turn, assumes the responsibility to learn and to study. If he fails in this, the university can fail him. In this respect, he is dependent on the considered expert judgment of the faculty much in the same way as the client or patient of a professional person subjects himself to the judgment of the practitioner who possesses a competence and an expertise which the customer lacks.

And as the skilled, wise, and secure practitioner will attempt to offer a freedom of choice among different alternatives, where and whenever pos-

38

ible, so the school must endeavor to leave within the educational program
hoices for student decision. These might consist of selection of the instruc-
or in courses with more than one section, of incorporating elective courses
nto the curriculum, or, depending on objectives and subject matter, of involving the students in the selection of specific topics for a given seminar
within an overall framework. Incidentally, this was written before I saw the
minutes of the Regional Student Conference, which call for the same oppor-
unities.

In a legal and formal sense, formulating, deciding upon, and approving
curriculum are functions that belong intrinsically and logically to faculty,
administration, and boards. These functions represent the core of educa-
ional responsibility and are, so to speak, the product for which the student
contracted. Practice, however, is not an exclusively academic enterprise. It
occurs outside the walls of the university and reflects the needs and currents
of the community. Since professional education is preparation for responsible entry into practice, it is, therefore, necessary and inevitable that curriculum and program construction be influenced by developments in prac-
ice, as well as those in theory.

It is in this context that the students, who are tomorrow's citizens and
practitioners, have an important role to play. What they have to say, what
they conceive as needs, what they see as the important issues of the future
is not insignificant. It might be incoherent, erroneous, and even misinformed, but it certainly is significant. We would do well to listen to and
consider what they have to say, and to assess its validity. This does not
mean full voting membership on the curriculum committee, but it is a far
cry from saying: "We have all the answers, and if they don't like it, they
can lump it." To me, it represents the essence of involvement—namely, responsible participation—and genuine give-and-take within the structure of
an institution composed of mature, sensible human beings, each playing his
proper role. Irving Howe states it well:

> What our most thoughtful and restless students are requesting is not that ac-
> ademic decisions be turned over to "student mobs," but that they be allowed,
> through democratic channels, to express their views about matters of greatest
> concern to them. Often enough students are wrong in their opinions about ac-
> ademic life and educational policy, but then, so are the rest of us; and a supply
> of fresh mistakes might be invigorating.[3]

It follows that there is a place for student involvement in curriculum development. Whether this takes place in the form of regular participation in
curriculum committees or representation on special occasions, through student surveys or questionnaires, depends on the situation in each individual
school. It is important that channels of communicating student reactions,
desires, and needs not only be established but used, that a sense of partnership be fostered without giving the impression of condescendence, a fatal

---

[3]Howe, *Ibid.,* p. xx.

quality for the creation of a sound, viable student-faculty relationship.

There are a number of educational programs in which students play an important part in planning and in execution. An example is the orientation program through which many schools introduce their incoming first-year class. School weekends or trips are another instance of joint planning and execution; often the major part of these ventures can and should be carried by the students. Each of us can, I am sure, think of other opportunities illustrating the different ways in which students participate in educational programs.

This has been a somewhat rambling and wide-ranging presentation which does not lend itself very readily to a concise summary. Instead, let me review a few points which I believe are basic to our discussion, and perhaps add a few final thoughts on the subject. I have no apologies for a position which strikes many as essentially conservative, but which, I hope, will not be considered as reactionary. I sincerely believe, because I have experienced its challenge and seen its effectiveness, that students have the right to become involved in the affairs of their school. I am not sure that we have solved the question of representation. Student bodies are not homogeneous; it is not always clear for whom the spokesman actually speaks. My impression is that the degree of representativeness varies in accordance with the nature of the issue under consideration. It certainly remains a problem for the students themselves, but is also very important for faculty and administration in their evaluation of the significance and validity of the matters presented to them. That involvement usually has to stop at the point of decision-making does not negate the process. Involvement must include all concerned parties and must mean more than just listening. It also cannot mean blind acceptance. It will not eliminate pain and discomfort—and therefore dissatisfaction—because learning to become a helping person and to use oneself in a professional relationship is painful and difficult. It will not produce universal agreement because it deals with issues on which there exist genuine differences of opinion. But it will help to provide a climate essential for the purpose of the joint enterprise in which we are all engaged: a more relevant and functional educational process through which students can learn, grow, and be challenged to bring the best in them to the foreground, and faculty will be stimulated to teach creatively, to be educators in the full meaning of the word. In this way, student power becomes an essential constructive force, and the "establishment" a responsible carrier of institutional and community power, both making possible "maximum feasible participation" in the pursuit of excellence, which is the essence and the rationale of the university.

EDUCATIONAL BASES FOR STUDENT INVOLVEMENT IN THE ADMINISTRATION OF SOCIAL WORK SCHOOLS

WINIFRED BELL

IT IS DOUBTFUL that any subject has been more exhaustively explored in recent years than the relationship between the student and the university. Many of the most penetrating thinkers of the nation, university administrators, and students, have discussed the problem, sometimes in solo efforts, as often in group confrontations. They have questioned the purpose of universities, their unique qualities as communities and social systems, and their function in society. The time-honored institution, the company of scholars, has been dissected and challenged, and concepts such as "relevance," "participatory democracy," "activist," "faculty tenure," "student power," and "youth revolt" have become common household terms.

The focus today is on educational bases or the rationale for student involvement in the administration of social work schools. For this purpose, administration is defined broadly to mean the processes of designing, planning, and implementing the educational system including the formal and informal relationships among various role partners who comprise the academic social work community—namely, governing groups such as trustees and boards, administrators, faculty, students, and field work supervisors.

There are others who also affect social work education, including the host university and community, the professional association, CSWE, alumni, educational funding sources, taxpayers, political leaders. There is also an extremely powerful and very old tradition, known as the university ethos, and a younger associate, known as academic freedom, that inform decision-making in important ways.

This is the cast of characters, a mixture of concepts, roles, and human beings who, ten or fifteen years back, appeared to live in obscure harmony

Reprinted from the Social Work Education Reporter, *Vol. 17, No. 4 (December, 1969), pp. 56-59.*

and, during this decade, have been plunged into violent conflict. True, the chaos has been more typical of undergraduates and large universities than of professional students or schools, but, for better or worse, what happens to the parent institution and its younger students cannot help but influence individual schools and older students. Since the wider public rarely makes such nice distinctions, constraints on host institutions tend to be replicated in their constituent parts, and mass emotions are contagious.

One anomaly in the vast flood of material on the subject is the relative neglect of the educational rationale for involving students. In the electric atmosphere of student revolt, attention has focused on the causes of protest, the attributes of protestors, the anatomy of universities, and types of surgery that might impede the course of violence. The preoccupation is with structure, rather than style, and with communication channels, rather than creative partnership. The effort appears to be directed most often toward appeasing a small but vociferous group who, some observers insist, wish to destroy universities as a symbol of a decadent society and use the obvious collectivities of youth to this end. But there is serious question as to whether this small nucleus could gain such widespread support, even temporarily, if there were not pervasive dissatisfactions with the educational experience, dissatisfactions which no attention to structure or communication will correct.

GOALS OF STUDENT INVOLVEMENT

1. Structural Representation

The problem can be illuminated by examining the assumptions that underlie the various approaches to student involvement. The most popular cliché is advanced by groups which appear to be heavily influenced by a wish for an equilibrium which can be interpreted as relatively akin to the status quo. They come to the bargaining table reluctantly, or with a heavy orientation toward ritualism or "me-tooism"; although, this is not to suggest that their viewpoint does not have merit. It goes to the effect that a university or professional school can only become a "true academic community," a phrase they rarely define, if it is a representative government in which the three groups, administration, faculty, and students, participate "fully" and "appropriately." Without being specific, they explain that a school or university is a social system of mutually interdependent roles with rights, responsibilities, obligations, and privileges. One of the obligations of administration is to make final decisions; to abrogate this obligation would be illegal. Of course, though, the advice of role partners should be sought. Administrators in such settings are often vigorously supported by professors who zealously guard their time-honored privilege of selecting and promoting colleagues and awarding academic tenure.

Superficially, this viewpoint sounds promising, given knowledge regarding the distribution of power in universities. At least, it generates a new or more viable structure: student representation on some or all committees, formal communication channels, an open-door policy for administrators, increased faculty time for individual conferences, and a more active student organization. The resulting structure can be neat and tidy. But there is no evidence yet that these structural shifts, by themselves, will improve the educational output, increase student satisfactions, or decrease explicit discontents.

It seems likely that preoccupation with structure neglects very crucial variables, including the subtle differences in executive style and their impact on the health, morale, and vitality of schools. It is noteworthy that exponents of the structural approach proclaim their wish to benefit from everyone's ideas while insisting that they have no obligation to reflect them in practice. To this vintage of administrator, this legalism is self-evident. But it is not at all self-evident to others. Committee participation is not necessarily synonymous with decision-making, a lesson all too patent in urban slum programs. So, if laws and regulations must be changed to legitimate a genuine sharing of power, the democratization of decision-making must also be accomplished.

Perhaps this goal can be hastened by exposing students with a high order of critical intelligence to the committee process. They might even ask some cogent questions that their elders avoid. No one is yet an authority on what actually occurs in committees in social work schools, why so many are necessary, or how or where vital decisions are made. But the grapevine suggests that there are too many committees that meet too frequently and accomplish too little. It is as though "togetherness" is a consistent virtue, and the bureaucratic ways of life in the social agency are more treasured than the university ethos. One can be a great admirer of appropriate structure and know that the failure to structure for success often leads to failure, and yet believe that the more vital variable is the quality of executive leadership. For the human grace and style of the man at the helm cannot help but have a pervasive influence on the health of the academic community, irrespective of its structural tidiness or its ritualistic bows to the committee process.

A beneficient executive style is not easily described. But it appears to include a combination of openness to adverse as well as favorable feedback, respect for faculty and student colleagues, appropriate reliance on professional and bureaucratic values as reference groups shift, ease in delegation, ability to recognize errors and shift in midstream, a flare and appreciation for the enabling role, a sense of humor, and the ability to plan systematically and carefully so that talents are well used and people are caught up in a drive toward excellence. This is a large order, but there are deans who bring this quality of leadership to schools, and their rewards are immediate and tangible: they attract and hold good staff despite limitations in physical resources or emoluments. In such settings, student participation in committees often proves fruitful and satisfying. But at the other extreme, participation may merely make inroads on scarce student time and generate more discontent and disillusion.

2. Experience in Participatory Democracy

The second rationale for involving students has to do with the virtues of participatory democracy as distinguished from representative government. In a nation so agonized over the alienation of too many of its youth, its poor, and its black citizens, the rediscovery of the town meeting has great attraction. Etzioni, in discussing student riots at Columbia University, noted that students and faculty in the sociology department comprised a sufficiently small number to make either highly centralized or representative government unnecessary for many purposes.[1] The groups could meet together and arrive at decisions. So, to the extent that schools remain fairly small or universities delegate or decentralize, students might gain an experience with direct democracy that could serve them throughout life in their roles as citizens, family members, and professionals. Learning not only the process but the constraints imposed by budgets and tradition could enrich education in important ways.

The appeal of this argument should be manifest for schools of social work where the social change role is part of the educational fare. But its relevance for many disciplines is advanced by scholars. Too much of the academic experience, it is held, has been in the service of tradition and conformity, and too little in the interest of social change.[2] Exponents of this view call attention to studies of student protestors. Two groups have been isolated. The first are the activists who tend to come from intellectual, professional families who have taken mental hygiene precepts seriously, have involved their children in vital decisions, given them many advantages, and encouraged curiosity and invention. Such youth arrive at universities with high expectations, considerable self-respect, and the confidence that their contribution is valuable. They are above average in achievement. Unlike the alienated youth who are also attracted to the protest movement, they are not sick, they do not reject their parents' values or goals, although they may act them out more courageously than was possible for their parents. They are not withdrawing from a mainstream they cannot or dare not try to join. The activists are reformers, who are credited with having brought about more improvement in universities in a few years than was witnessed in decades.[3]

[1]Amatai Etzioni, "Confession of a Professor Caught in a Revolution," *New York Times* Magazine Section, September 15, 1968. Also see Nathan Tarcov, "The Last Four Years at Cornell," *The Public Interest,* Fall, 1968.

[2]Kenneth B. Clark, "Intelligence, the University and Society," *The American Scholar,* Winter, 1966-67; James W. Trent and Judith L. Craise, "Commitment and Conformity in the American College," *Journal of Social Issues,* July, 1967; Henry David, "Education for the Professions," *Journal of Education for Social Work,* Spring, 1967.

[3]Kenneth Keniston, "The Sources of Student Dissent," *Journal of Social Issues,* July, 1967; Edward E. Sampson, "Student Activism and the Decade of Protest," *Ibid.*; Richard E. Peterson, "The Student Left in American Higher Education," *Daedalus,* Winter, 1968; Seymour Martin Lipset, "The Activists: A Profile," *The Public Interest,* Fall, 1968.

Jencks and Riesman have illumined this subject in their recent work, *The Academic Revolution*.[4] Universities, they testify, have not been conspicuous searchers after truth nor noteworthy social critics. Instead, the great lowering of higher education in the 19th century in the United States had the effect and goal of checking social change. The consequence today is an overweening conformity and credentialism which presume, without proof, to produce an excellent educational output.

Participatory democracy may provoke great resistance in academia where students outnumber faculty. Or it may seem like a pious hope rather than a practical possibility. Whether or not attendance at the town meeting in early New England guaranteed or even facilitated democratic participation of all role partners, reports out of Massachusetts in recent years suggest that even when towns remain small and attendance at official meetings is encouraged, decision-making is not necessarily democratic, let alone productive of an adaptive response to changed conditions. People arrive with different commitments, different experience, more or less knowledge of the issues and their background and consequences, and hence they command different degrees of power in the marketplace of persuasion.

Beyond these variables, the length of stay differs radically among role partners in the academic setting, and in the professional schools, senior faculty are very important to students who look forward to good jobs in the profession. Indeed, Sidney Hook is so impressed by the resulting wish to please their professors and "mentors" that his solution for campus riots is to use senior faculty as the primary negotiators.[5] The question, some scholars believe, is whether pressures toward conformity do not already exact too high a price for student and society alike.[6] The need in professional schools, they insist, is to free students so that they can afford to be frank, without fear of reprisal. To achieve such a milieu, deans and faculty must develop the ability to forego praise in favor of truth and honesty, to scorn and see through the suspect loyalty oath, and to react to the quality, not the source, of comment. If schools of social work could help experiments in direct democracy to succeed, everyone involved would benefit as they learned to move together in critically important efforts to reshape and revitalize institutions, for nowhere is there an institutional structure more permeated with problems than in social welfare.

3. *Qualitative Improvement in Education*

The third rationale for student involvement is that participation in decisions vitally affecting a person improves his morale, productivity, and the

---

[4]Christopher Jencks and David Riesman, *The Academic Revolution* (New York: Doubleday, 1968); also see John William Ward, "Cleric or Critic: The Intellectual in the University," *The American Scholar,* Winter, 1965-66.

[5]Sidney Hook, "Hook Favors Bigger Role for Faculty," *The New York Times,* September 8, 1968.

[6]Christopher Bay, "Political and Apolitical Students: In Search of Theory," *Journal of Social Issues,* July, 1967; Martin Duberman, "An Experiment in Education," *Daedalus,* Winter, 1968; Samuel Lubell, "That 'Generation Gap,' " *Public Interest,* Fall, 1968.

quality of his output.[7] Exponents of this view draw attention to how little is known about morale in academia or the quality of the educational output Universities are judged by a series of inputs: courses of study, educational degrees of faculty and their scholarly publications, teacher-student ratios, salary ranges, physical plant including library volumes, high school grade averages of students, and the like. But very little is known about the sub-substance and flow of courses or their relevance, or the style of teaching and its success in awakening youth and encouraging intellectual search, or even the relative strengths of graduates of various universities.[8]

Scholars who favor student involvement because of its potential for improving morale, productivity, or quality return repeatedly to the classroom as the important arena for involvement. Would students be so disenchanted if all was well in the classroom? What goal convergence is there between instructors and students? What makes the great professor? Will any amount or kind of student influence in the management of schools or universities suffice unless classroom style, manners, and content are enriched and restructured?

The sad truth, according to some authorities, is that most teachers are un-inspired people who simply work for a living and have no wish to be stimulated to greater investment of time, energy, or spirit. They assign basic textbooks and then summarize them for students. They may update bibliographies, although even this is not certain, but they rarely reorganize or reconceptualize courses or move to discard them entirely. They do too little individual thinking, and when they become involved in research they too often exploit their tangential interests to the neglect of the mainstream of ideas. They give examinations which require regurgitation of their outlines and viewpoints. They rarely refurbish their intellectual household or re-examine its foundations. So they inevitably prepare students for the past rather than the future, to the extent that they prepare them for anything but the sheepskin.[10]

But their primary sin is their arrogance in assuming that they are there solely to teach and to correct and students are there solely to learn and to admire. What they overlook is that their audience is at the most creative age in the life span, and even short of creative imagination, may include individuals with special talents, experiences, and knowledge which could

[7]Kurt Lewin, "Group Decision and Social Change," in Eleanor E. Maccoby, Theodore M Newcomb, and Eugene L. Hartley (eds.), Readings in Social Psychology (New York: Holt Rinehart & Winston, Inc., 1958). This source shows effect on morale and productivity; references to quality permeate the literature.

[8]Paul Woodring, The Higher Learning in America (New York: McGraw-Hill, 1968).

[9]Frank C. Jennings, "The Savage Rage of Youth," Saturday Review, June 15, 1968; Kenneth Keniston, "American Students and 'Political Revival,' " The American Scholar, Winter, 1962-63.

[10]Jennings, op. cit.; Harold Howe II, quoted in Saturday Review, September 15, 1968, p. 66; Martin Duberman, "Exploring Academia," The New Republic, June 22, 1968; John William Ward, op. cit.

omplement their own and immeasurably assist in the development of the mutually stimulating milieu without which inspired classroom experiences arely occur.

When students arrive in professional schools heavily indoctrinated by ears of passive ingestion and superficial conformity, and when advising procedures and field work experiences in those schools reinforce dependence and conformity, it may be and often is difficult to convince them that ree and adventuresome involvement is actually the classroom goal. It is lso incredibly difficult to sustain such an ethos when universities rely so heavily on required courses, objective examinations, and grading systems. But it is not impossible, as many gifted teachers prove yearly.[11]

One of the exciting phenomena of the times is the steady rise in student xpectations. It makes the older generation acutely aware of the passage of time, for it never occurred to many of us that a teacher owed us anything. This may be why so few gifted teachers were encountered along the way. In my experience the size of the class, the physical facilities, or the subject vere not the crucial variables. Uniformly, the gifted teachers had high expectations, a delight in ideas, especially if they came from the young, inquiring and fertile minds, and they were deeply involved in professional, scholarly, or community pursuits which they called upon constantly to enrich their teaching.

But today's students more often than not expect excellence and are outraged or insulted by its opposite. This is most heartening in a society which needs all of the talented manpower it can develop if solutions to complex problems are to be found in time. Indeed, this was part of Alfred Whitehead's concern when he provided the rationale, years ago, for student involvement in the classroom. The educational dilemma flowed, he observed, from the fact that the young were imaginative but inexperienced, while the old were experienced but unimaginative. What was needed was a genuine creative partnership between the two in the search for truth an excellence.[12]

The question is no longer whether students should participate, but where, how, and to what extent and purpose, and how this involvement can enrich, not detract from the educational experience. The right of service consumers to influence services is a cardinal principle of this decade. It is a most promising idea for bringing about reform and improvement in the institutional structure and enhancing the quality of life. Irving Kristol's recent suggestion for funneling federal funds for higher education solely into student stipends is in this spirit.[13] With real freedom of choice, students could

---

[11]Among the more interesting among many articles on the subject is William R. Hutchison, Yes, John, There are Teachers on the Faculty," *The American Scholar,* Summer, 1966.

[12]Lucian Price, *Dialogues of Alfred North Whitehead* (Boston: Little, Brown and Co., 1954), assim.

[13]Irving Kristol, "A Different Way to Restructure the University," *The New York Times* Magazine Section, December 8, 1968.

47

vote with their feet for the universities and schools that met their expectations. Conversely, there would be a yardstick for identifying marginal or ineffective schools which failed to attract sufficient students.

The present dangers, short of this solution, are that most students will be too busy, too compliant, or too indifferent to take their opportunity seriously, or that they will be deluded into thinking that representation on committees is an inevitable prelude to reform. These are the impediments that have caused many serious efforts to increase democratic participation to fall short or fail. But as in the areas of race relations or urban affairs, money or structural innovations will never accomplish precious goals. Students can join committees *ad nauseum* and *ad infinitum,* sacrificing costly time from their educational budget. But the forward look and quality that we yearn for will more probably depend on leaders and teachers who are first and foremost, human beings with spacious minds and a reviving fount of goodwill and integrity, honesty and flexibility, good humor, humility, and imagination. It is axiomatic that for this type of individual, students are the natural allies, and that the protest of youth against outmoded institutions, anachronistic values, and mediocrity will ever be a cause for rejoicing.

STUDENT INVOLVEMENT: PARTICIPATORY DEMOCRACY OR ADULT SOCIALIZATION?

F. J. PEIRCE

STUDENTS, faculty, administration, the profession, and the community all have crucial responsibilities in the development of policy in schools of social work. Unfortunately, until recently little has been done to develop clarity of role, authority, and responsibility of the parties involved. This role confusion has been most apparent regarding the status of students, in particular, and, by implication, of faculty. This paper is an effort to suggest some guidelines with particular emphasis on the student role in the development of school policy.

In the present discussions, negotiations, and confrontations related to student participation in policy- and decision-making in schools of social work, one thing is quite clear; social work educators emphasize and place a high value on the process of student socialization.

> Academic institutions exist for the transmission of knowledge, the pursuit of truth, the development of students, and the general well-being of society.[1]

Of the four purposes noted in this statement, it seems that the moral and emotional development of students, or student socialization, has been valued most and has received the major emphasis. In large measure, this emphasis has resulted from the failure of social work educators in the classroom and in the field to recognize and value the student as anything more than a "young life" or potential recruit to be molded into some preferred image for "responsible entry into practice." The preferred "package" may be stated implicitly or explicitly. More often than not, it would appear that the decision-making process is covert and that the desired model is subtly hidden in egalitarian verbiage dedicated to the search for truth and the development of creative and innovative systems.

---

[1] "Joint Statement on Rights and Freedoms of Students," *AAUP Bulletin,* Vol. 53, No. 4 (Winter, 1967), p. 365.

Reprinted from the Journal of Education for Social Work, *Vol. 6, No. 2 (Fall, 1970), pp. 21-26.*

It appears, with some exceptions, that the student is not valued as a person who can, in any significant way, contribute to the processes of policy- and decision-making. Bell has noted in a sound and honest manner that student participation in administration of schools of social work is usually related to one or more of three goals: structural representation, experience in participatory democracy, and qualitative improvement of education.[2] Except for the last, these have little relevance to the quality of service or practice.

Ripple has studied and succinctly summarized the participatory models used by schools of social work as of the fall of 1968:

> Three major groupings were found in terms of administrative structure (1) activity is through the *student* organization; (2) there is a single, overall joint *student-faculty* committee; and (3) students are members of one or more *faculty committees.* [Emphasis mine.][3]

At best, these models result in a process which emphasizes the "rites of passage," or the adult socialization process. At worst, they result in adversary proceedings. In between these two extremes exists a certain amount of rather dull committee and group process focused on informing members of meeting times and changes, agenda, and the litigious intricacies of voting procedures. In the absence of charismatic leadership, what emerges most often from such groups is quite bland, consisting in large measure of the least offensive compromise acceptable to all, with occasional bows in the direction of educational quality and integrity.

There are many factors implicated in the monumental problems faced by the profession and its educators in attempting to improve the quality of education. One of these is the failure to recognize honestly and to place great value and operational emphasis on the core or root role of the student as a colleague in a community of learners. It is the thesis of this paper that acceptance of this philosophical and role perspective would facilitate the quest for educational and service excellence and minimize much unnecessary conflict. Far too much time is presently wasted on establishing and evaluating structures and procedures for "student involvement." Too much of this is based on barely hidden assumptions of student inferiority instead of recognition that students, like faculty, bring a wide range of interests, abilities, and potentialities for positive participation and contributions.

> The present generation of young people in our universities is the best informed, the most intelligent, and the most idealistic. . . . It is also the most sensitive to public issues and the most sophisticated in political tactics. . . .

---

[2]Winifred Bell, "Educational Bases for Student Involvement in the Administration of Social Work Schools," *Social Work Education Reporter,* Vol. 17, No. 4 (December, 1969), pp 56-59. Also, *supra,* pp. 41-49.

[3]Lilian Ripple, "Students' Rights and Responsibilities in Graduate Schools of Social Work: Survey of Current Practice," *Social Work Education Reporter,* Vol. 17, No. 2 (June, 1969), p. 48. Also, *supra,* pp. 13-20.

. . . today's students take seriously the ideals taught in schools and churches, and often at home, and then they see a system that denies its ideals in its actual life.[4]

Instead of capitalizing on the potential noted above, social work educators have continued to emphasize the social and educational benefits to students resulting from their participation and have in general neglected to accept them as individual equals in school policy-making. This paper is not a plea for equality of students and faculty. Rather it is a plea for the democratic principle that all participants have equal individual status in appropriate areas of the decision-making process. This does not mean that students will or should "run the schools." It does invest integrity and value in their contributions at least equal to that of other decision-making participants. This principle negates the practice of hearing students, as it were, during the "children's hour," and then proceeding to the important business at hand when they are gone. It is honestly recognized that some student participants are and will be immature, uninformed, rash, and judgmental; in short, that they will possess the same attributes of most faculty groups. Fortunately for all, both groups include persons who are intelligent, sensitive, committed to educational and service excellence, and who evidence regular capacity to translate these qualities into meaningful activity with significant results.

Too much current thinking is devoted to recognizing the limitations and problems of student participation. One such commentary notes that students need, "more than a 'hearing' or an outlet for the expression of opinion . . . ,"[5] and goes on to note that this may be ". . . incoherent, erroneous and even misinformed. . . ."[6] However, the concession is made that "there is a place for student involvement. . . ."[7] Examples provided of appropriate student roles in such a process include developing orientation programs, school weekends, or trips.[8] This classic elaboration of the induction or initiation model concludes with the suggestion that because ". . . involvement usually has to stop at the point of decision-making does not negate the process."[9] It is this devotion to the value of process rather than to values derived from democratic philosophy which most clearly results in the failure to develop responsible and meaningful participation by students.

---

[4] *Crisis at Columbia: Report of the Fact-Finding Commission Appointed to Investigate the Disturbances at Columbia University in April and May 1968* (New York: Vintage Books, 1968), p. 4.

[5] Paul Schreiber, "Student Involvement in Administration and Policy Formation and Educational Programs and Curriculum Development," *Social Work Education Reporter*, Vol. 6, No. 4 (December, 1968), p. 55. Also, *supra*, pp. 31-41.

[6] *Ibid.*, p. 58.

[7] *Ibid.*, p. 67.

[8] *Ibid.*

[9] *Ibid.*, p. 67.

Several principles are crucial in the development of structures and processes for policy-making in schools of social work. Since faculty are accountable to society, the profession, and universities for educational quality, they have ultimate responsibility for educational policy-making. Students, as significant representatives of society, the profession, and the university, must be involved in policy-making at all levels, including final decisions. Final responsibility for personnel decisions must rest with school administrators as they are held accountable for faculty quality and performance. However, students and faculty must be involved in key roles in the formulations of personnel policies and decisions.

With the above in mind it would appear that the most effective policy making structure would be one which could be described as an open and public system. This would mean that students would serve on all committees with full membership status. It would mean that faculty meetings would generally be public, with student representatives participating with full status. Exceptions to the open and public rule must be clearly defined in advance and should involve only those matters of confidentiality wherein individual student or faculty privacy must be protected.

The most efficient system would appear to be one in which matters to be considered in faculty meetings would be first studied and evaluated by appropriate school committees. Recommendations from committees or special task forces should be the primary focus of faculty meetings.

It should be clear that this perspective represents an effort to clarify and emphasize the prerogatives of all involved in the social work educational enterprise. Clarity of this sort may well be needed in some schools where the rights and duties of faculty and administration, as well as students, are not clear and generally rest on the authority of tradition, social status, and the grading system.

A key concept in this perspective is that of "full membership status" for students on school committees. This perspective represents something more than "full voting rights." To be allowed to vote, while an essential component, is but one element of "full status" on a policy-making body. There are other significant features involved in full membership status. These include first and foremost a group value orientation which accords each individual member equal beginning position and, thus, power in terms of that body's deliberations and actions. It means, to use what may be a trite phrase, the recognition that student members with full membership status are not "second-class" participants allowed to play "SIM-SOC" with simulated power, prestige, and position, but who must be carefully excluded from the real-life games played by the "big kids."[10] This would mean, for example, that students would have equal access to vital information and data on which decisions are based. It would mean that meetings would be scheduled to facilitate participation of all members, including

---

[10]William A. Gamson, *Sim Soc: Simulated Society* (New York: The Free Press, 1969).

ing students. It would not preclude pre-committee caucuses to develop plans and stragegies to achieve preferred results by blocs of members organizing together on the basis of ideas. It would, however, preclude "bat roost" faculty caucuses of the "grown-ups" before the agreed-upon decisions are taken in the "official" meetings.

Corollary to these examples of the rights of full membership status are the duties which are also a part of such a role. These may include sharing the fact-finding or secretarial chores and might even mean that some poor unsuspecting student will find himself holding the dubious "honor" of chairing a committee. All full members would also share in the responsibility for decisions, taken, thus denying to students, as well as to faculty, the "bat roost" game as well as the role of outraged minority.

Most discussions of student involvement bog down over the meaning of the concept of policy-making. Some have suggested student and faculty participation at "all operational levels." The issue is not the straw man of participation at "all operational levels." A completely "open participation" policy would be impossible to maintain in any operation, although many school faculties have operated in this manner, with regard to openness of "operational groups" to all other faculty. Fortunately, most faculty and students have little interest in attending the multitude of operational meetings held at various levels and for innumerable purposes. It is very likely that if all of these meetings were open, few would wish to attend once the aura of secrecy and mysticism was destroyed by exposure to the vapid realities of process in such sessions.

Rather than limiting discussion and recommendations to the policy-making and operational level dichotomy, it is important to recognize a key intermediate level, that of interpretive decision-making based on policy. This particular process is what finally results in operational-level activities and not the prior decisions made at the policy level.

Thus, the three levels of *potential* participation for all members of the community of a school of social work may be seen as:

1. Policy-making
2. Interpretive decision-making based on policy
3. Operational activities resulting from decision-making

The first level involves many who are outside of the immediate school community, such as advisory boards, graduate divisions, university administrators, and boards of trustees. Closer to the school community are other significant groups which must be involved at this level, such as practitioners, field instructors, alumni, and even those who will be the recipients of social work service.

The second level of decision-making is one of those "gray areas" that social work educators are so fond of recognizing. Unfortunately, recognition is seldom followed by efforts to clarify the situation but too often by exhortations to avoid swinging the pendulum too far in either direction or the equally over-used cliché about maintaining a tight grip on some tiresome baby who is always in danger of being washed down the drain. It may be questionable whether much clarity will result from this paper, but the effort must be made.

Obviously, students must participate in the school community with full membership status at the policy-making level. It is just as clear that their participation at the operational level will only add to the present bureaucratic chaos observed in much of the day-to-day administrative activity of many schools. There are already too many simple administrative activities with an unnecessary abundance of reluctant participants. The committees on scholarship awards and field assignment are probably the best examples of this conspicuous consumption of operational activities. Policy regarding these functions should be clear. Interpretive decisions should be made as to the operational criteria for awards and assignments and the implications of the policy should be fully spelled out. Then, one person should carry out the operational activity, returning to the interpretive level only when problems which do not fit the criteria present themselves. It might be noted that, given clarity at the first two levels, the third may often be carried out by a competent secretary or administrative assistant.

Because the second level of interpretive decision-making determines the meaning of policy, students should participate with full membership status on these school decision-making bodies. More of these groups exist in the school community than those at the other levels and their activities are most crucial in determining the full value and meaning of social work education. It is at this level that the validity and integrity of a policy is determined and democratic imperatives once again require student participation.

The philosophy outlined here clearly implies that policy-making bodies should be identified and should perform as school committees and not as faculty committees. This is not intended to neglect the necessity for segregated groups organized on the basis of the functional duties, needs, and special interests. Certainly, for example, most schools need to devote some exclusive faculty attention to faculty development and improvement. Students might well be invited to help with this, but the major responsibility and interest should be from faculty and administration. Other special interests of the various groups in the school community could be noted. The significant principle is, however, not related to the particular needs of the separate identifiable groups but the importance of the value placed on those broad representative groups which are significant to the life and process of the school community. These should not be known as faculty or as faculty-student committees, but as school or even school-community committees so it will be clear that no one group participates at the sufferance of another.

Discussions of this sort often include a plea for granting educational credit for student participation in school policy-making. This would appear to negate the value of student contribution and emphasize again the socializing and learning quality of the experiences. It must further be recognized that much participation is, indeed, not educational and, it might be inferred, not even beneficial to the student or other participants. It is true that faculty get "paid" for committee participation, but one would risk instant annihilation if it were suggested that the recompense is often satisfactory or directly related to the effort, pain, and tedium required. The plea for student credit is frequently an effort to make participation more attractive. This is probably a social and physical impossibility. It appears that students will have to decide if the end merits suffering the means. It is to be hoped that the response will be an affirmative one. This conviction is held, despite the fear of charges that this belief will lead the unsuspecting down some primrose path to self-punishment and catatonia.

The number of student participants on policy or interpretive bodies is directly related to their potential for positive contributions. No plea will be made here for magic formulae or ratios. This is too simplistic and fails to recognize the variation in the needs, strengths, and problems of the different schools, faculties, and student groups. The number of students, faculty, and others on each committee should be determined by the nature of the committee and not by some arbitrary formula which posits superior wisdom and expertise to faculty or students. Thus, a committee on students, as such, might well have a majority of students and one dealing with faculty development, a faculty majority. A single student member on a committee is easily isolated or bullied in subtle ways. Further, he may find that he is not trusted by his peers when he returns to report to them. A minimum of at least two is required, if for no other reasons than to avoid isolation and convert intimidation, as well as to keep the student participants honest with their constituency. The pattern of one representative each from the first- and second-year classes represents some improvement over that of a single member representing both classes. The potential exists that the same problems may occur resulting from separation and isolation of the two classes and the possibility that the second-year student, who has been well socialized, will join in the process of initiating and intimidating his junior colleague. For these reasons, it would seem preferable to have more than one member from both classes if this can be done without creating a committee which is no longer a group but a convention.

Other problems related to numbers and membership tenure arise. Faculty will almost always have seniority on a given school committee. This may result in negative attitudes because of the requirement that faculty bring the new members up to date on group goals, activities, and processes. This problem can never be fully overcome, but a positive improvement might result from two-year membership by student participants.

55

The goal of this paper has been to demonstrate the operational implica tions in the profession's dedication to democratic values. Some issues have not been covered. One such issue concerns the boundaries of student par ticipation with respect to personal of confidential information as well as with faculty personnel practices. In terms of confidentiality of personal in formation, the same principles apply here as in other activities. The most crucial of these is that an organization should hold as little personal infor mation as is absolutely needed for its successful operation. That which is held should be shared only with those who have an operational need for it. When the information is no longer useful to anyone, it should be de stroyed.

In conclusion, student participation is now a fact and not some distant goal. Discussions of this nature can no longer be focused on whether or even when this participation will take place. Instead, they must focus on the value system which underlies such participation and how this will be translated into effective and meaningful participation which is congruent with the avowed values of the profession and its educational system.

STUDENT PARTICIPATION IN DECISION-MAKING IN SCHOOLS OF SOCIAL WORK

JOSEPH L. VIGILANTE

SOCIAL WORK EDUCATION for several years has become increasingly sensitive to the changes in student-faculty-administrative roles in the universities. This article is concerned with the relationships between the current social revolution, the student revolution, the university system, and schools of social work. It attempts to assess the current status of decision-making in social work education within a "revolutionary" context and to identify the associated patterns and trends. The author views the present dialogues and conflicts between students, administrators, and faculty essentially as a process of power transfer. This article is based upon the experience of an administrator in a school of social work who has participated in the transfer process and who is also a member of "The Committee on Students" of the Council on Social Work Education. It is one man's impression (retrospective and current) of the tumultuous years between 1966 and 1970, and it is submitted as one point of view, among many, toward encouraging a necessary, continuing examination of the changing roles of students, faculty, and administrators.[1]

THE REVOLUTION

Although social work students have rarely *initiated* militant university-wide protests or "revolutionary" endeavors, their modes of protest within schools of social work often reflect the contemporary revolutionary mood.

[1]The author began writing this article in March, 1970. The writing was interrupted *and influenced by* the outbreak of the National Student Strike beginning May 5, 1970, in response to the escalation of the Southeast Asian War into Cambodia, the killing of four college students at Kent State University in Ohio, the killing of six black men in Augusta, Georgia, disorders a week later, and the killing of two black students on the campus of Jackson State College, Mississippi, a week later.

Reprinted from the Journal of Education for Social Work, *Vol. 6, No. 2 (Fall, 1970), pp. 51-60.*

There is ample evidence that the response of faculties and administrato in schools of social work has, for the most part, been accepting. This autho favors such a posture. However, understanding the issues around studen militancy and the pressure which the revolutionary phenomenon places o students, faculty, and administrators requires candid acceptance of the con temporary social-academic revolution as a political reality with irreversib outcomes for the future of the university as well as the society. There wi probably be no return to "normalcy" as we have known it. We will be livin in a vastly different academic environment with respect to university gov ernance as well as the conduct of the educational mission.

Even minimal experience in responding to students' dissatisfactions re veals that their concerns and the nature of their participation in on-campu problem-solving are directly related to and influenced by the character o the revolution. The revolution is youth-oriented. Youth in revolt revea special characteristics; namely, a dissatisfaction with past experience, rejection of history, impatience with process and "timing" in moving to ward change, a bias toward existential emphasis in social analysis, and tacit assumption that those holding authority or power *(per se)* are th potential enemy. The older generation, the power structure, and the mil tary-industrial complex are often lumped together as the target.[2] This pos tion has been articulated by the radical student leadership publicly. A though it is not affirmed by social work students in the same manner (ex cept in rare instances), it seems to be assumed by some student social wor leaders.

The university has been identified by the ultra-left radical student move ment as a tool of the military-industrial complex. The revolution denies th legitimacy[3] of contemporary social institutions including (and particularly the institution of higher education. The revolutionary, when forced, can an often does retreat to the claim that the university is illegitimate. He, there fore, is not subject to its rules. Again, many students, although they do no articulate this position, act in accordance with it in negotiations aroun their own demands. The rejection of societal rules for a belief that indivic

---

[2]The military-industrial complex is a term so overworked that it is in danger of losing bo its meaning and its significance. The term is used here in the sense that is conveyed by Jo Kenneth Galbraith, quoting Dwight Eisenhower, in his book, *The New Industrial State:* "T 'conjunction of an immense military establishment and a large arms industry' was somethi new in the American experience and urged that the nation 'guard against the acquisition unwarranted influence, whether sought or unsought, by the military industrial complex. T potential for the disastrous rise of misplaced power exists and will persist . . . we should ta nothing for granted.' " *The New Industrial State* (Boston, Mass.: Houghton Mifflin Co., 196 p. 331. Galbraith further develops this concept in a small pamphlet, *How to Control the M itary* (Garden City, N. Y.: Doubleday and Co., Inc., 1969).

[3]The terms of legitimacy and illegitimacy are used profusely in the literature of "the mov ment." The meaning of the term goes to the root of our present social dilemmas. It implies t well-known conflict between articulated values and social-institutional actualities. Moreove it specifies the gap between professional purpose and actual function. Within the terms (leg imacy-illegitimacy) lies one of the basic rationales for the present revolution.

uals must act in accordance with their own consciences encourages impulsive and intolerant decision-making. Not bound by a parliamentarian, legislative-like process, instant change can be expected. The quick, impulsive mood of revolution is antithetical to the deliberate and process-dominated procedures traditional in higher education and especially in professional education and practice.

Arguments for and about the participation of students in decision-making in schools of social work eventually bring out the issue of the sharing of power (or a part of it) with students. Social work educators anticipated quite early that students have a right to participation in decision-making, a right to some power. But in spite of this early recognition, and whether or not it is true of most schools of social work, it seems apparent that those who have power give it up reluctantly and only after constant harassment and irritation. When the harassment subsides and the pressure is off, the power is often repossessed. There is, on the other hand, some evidence that "the power structure" would rather give up some of its authority than experience the discomfort of trying to keep it.[4] If this is generally true, it is the single consoling phenomenon as yet observed by this writer in an otherwise depressing social climate.

As the process of power sharing has been underway in the university exemplified by student participation on faculty governing bodies and committees, we have witnessed suppressive reactions from off-campus centers of power. Through legislation and administrative regulations, the political decision-makers have demonstrated their dissatisfaction with the course of events on the campuses. In New York in 1969, all colleges and universities were required by a legislative act to file with the State Department of Education statements indicating lists of offenses and punishments with respect to student and/or faculty disruptions on the campus.[5] Currently, the governor of California is sponsoring legislation to suspend or expel academic dissenters. In 1969, federal regulations were established which would deny federal funds to students who were found guilty of disrupting academic programs.[6] While these forms of suppression have been directed against the constituents of academic institutions, we are also aware of a series of

---

[4]"The Politics of Protest," in "A Round-up of Current Research," *Transaction,* Vol. 7, No. 4 (February, 1970), p. 11.

[5]Assembly Bill 6610-a Article 129-a of the New York State Education Law Provides that "the trustees of every college chartered by the Regents shall adopt rules and regulations for the maintenance of public order on college campuses and other college property used for educational purposes and provide a program for the enforcement thereof." These rules apply to students, faculty, staff, visitors, invitees, and licensees on these campuses.

[6]Section 907 of the Department of Health, Education, and Welfare Appropriation Act of 1968 (P.L. 90-132) provides: "No part of the funds appropriated under this Act shall be used to provide payments, assistance, or services, in any form, with respect to any individual convicted in any Federal, State, or local court of competent jurisdiction, of inciting, promoting, or carrying on a riot, or any group activity resulting in material damage to property or injury to persons, found to be in violation of Federal, State, or local laws designed to protect persons or property in the community concerned."

suppressive measures which have been taking place in the broader societ These, too, are a part of the reaction to the social revolution and, of cours have their effect upon campus activities. I am referring to the emphasis o new social control instruments established in the Department of Justice, th move toward a strongly conservative U.S. Supreme Court, the offensiv misuse of justice in the trial of the Chicago Seven, as well as the genera treatment of the Black Panther Party in the United States. Both in the la enforcement agencies and in the courts the chronicle of suppression is grow ing longer by the month.[7]

It is not surprising, therefore, that student leadership has become in creasingly suspicious and distrusting of administrators. Still, many ac ademic administrators remain well identified with the intrinsic merit c power sharing. They themselves are often at odds with decision-makers o the campus. But university administrators, including deans and directors c schools of social work, are finding it difficult to maintain an accepting an yielding posture in the face of mounting distrust. It is difficult to be place in a position of suspicion as one attempts to negotiate with student leader ship requesting participation in decision-making. Students continually in sist that administrators *demonstrate* they can be trusted. Many student in graduate schools of social work today have had years of experience i negotiating with university administrators at the undergraduate level. Thei distrust, therefore, can be understood. It is within this climate of tension anger, hostility, and distrust, that the sharing of power is negotiated. Th current negative political climate, the tension created by evidence of polit ical suppression, has aggravated and exacerbated the already difficult pro cess of power transfer.

STRUCTURAL GUARANTEES

The atmosphere of distrust which characterizes student-faculty-administra tion negotiations contributes toward another phenomenon: the desire fo *structural guarantees* of student rights and due process. *Students want i in writing.* Professional values and professional ethics are not viewed a sufficient guarantees that their rights will be protected. It should be noted that even when the indicators of distrust are at their lowest level, the quie adamant insistence on organizational and structural change to guarantee due process and student rights continues. One cannot refrain from observ ing that guarantees in writing rather than trust in the good intentions and moral imperatives of professional or democratic efforts—the Bill of Rights o

[7]It is not difficult to document the evidence of suppression. A daily reading of the New York Times is sufficient. See, for example: Jack Rosenthal, "Experts Reject Plan of Ex-Nixo Doctor for Tests of Children to Find Potential Criminality," April 11, 1970, p. 15; B. Drum mond Ayers, Jr., "Agnew Urges Aid for Best Students," April 14, 1970, p. 30; J. Anthon Lukas, "Boston Police Raid Investigated," May 15, 1970, p. 1; Paul K. Benedict, Letter t the Editor, "Purged Scholar," May 15, 1970; Editorial, "Suppressing Rationality," May 15 1970, p. 32. Also see "WBAI" in "Talk of the Town," *New Yorker,* March 7, 1970.

e United States Constitution, the sanctity of contract as interpreted his-
orically in the United States Supreme Court, the repeated emphasis on
ritten covenants—are in the best tradition of classical western liberalism.
ule by law and not by man has been the major by-product of this historical,
hilosophical trend. We are, however, in danger of destroying the value of
ne principle of rule by law in the face of other behaviors which, at times,
lso characterize the revolution. The pattern of refusing to abide by ma-
ority decisions, the insistence of the right of the minority not merely to be
ifferent in peace but to disrupt the action of the majority are countervail-
ng contemporary behaviors.

HE BLACK MOVEMENT

A separate and significant factor influencing power sharing is the affect of
ne black social movement both off the campus and within the schools. For
ne black movement demands its own piece of power. Blacks have learned
ne prime lesson of negotiation, namely, that one does not negotiate the sys-
em except from a power base. Thus, the movement for special identifica-
on of black student organizations, with special kinds of inputs and special-
zed communication with school administrations. The black movement it-
elf is checkered with a variety of theories and influences, all of which can
e operating in the same school of social work at the same time with vary-
ng degrees of intensity. Educators, therefore, are faced with the dilemma of
he validity of black identification based on a philosophy of pluralism and
he recognition of the unique character of the black experience in America
on the one hand, and the need to maintain communication linkages with all
tudents on the other. Special and necessary relationships with black stu-
ent and faculty organizations create new stresses on the relationships be-
ween administration and other faculty and students. One of the common
haracteristics of problematic communications is that often one group of
tudents is not familiar with what another group has been doing or the
aculty may not be familiar with commitments made by the administration
nd/or vice versa. This writer is convinced that "communications" prob-
ems *do not stem* from inept administrative structures, or the lack of face-to-
ace contact between students, faculty, and administration. It is doubtful
hat a daily "newsletter" (a simplistic remedy too often resorted to) in-
reases communication. Unfortunately, the problem is probably the reality
of the differences existing between the many actors in the academic scene.
When the ultimate truth of the necessity to have more power is faced with
he need to retain power, positions become hardened and communication
obliterated. Dialogue assumes a readiness to yield on both sides. The ad-
ersary tradition in western systems of justice and debate does not en-
ourage softening in negotiation. The adversary system places primary im-
ortance on convincing your opponent or a referee (judge) that you are

right. Heuristic approaches to difference are rare, but absolutely necessary. A heuristic system assumes that the purpose of negotiation is for the parties to discover what is right together.

IDENTITIES AND ALLIANCES

Schools of social work in which faculty participation in decision-making has been the norm seem to find it easier to work out systems for sharing power than do those schools where the faculty as a body have been less involved in decision-making. In schools where faculties have not had a major role in decision-making, the student demands tend to reinforce alienated relationships between faculty and administrators. Administrators in these schools seem to find the growth of student power more disturbing while the faculties find it less so. Thus, it seems that in some schools there develops a relatively strong faculty-student identification while in others the student-administration identity may be stronger. The problem is further complicated where single faculties are split between those who have been participating in decision-making and those who have not. Polarized faculties often court or are courted by factions of students. The danger of each using the other for its own interest cannot be discounted. The effects of a change from a dyad relationship to a triad relationship (with the addition of students as a power group) cannot be underestimated as one views these interrelationships in a dynamic sense. The third party permits unprecedented opportunities for alliances (two against one), with the inevitable need to develop political strategies. Student leaders also, increasingly sensitized to the dynamic functioning of institutions, are rapidly gaining skills in negotiation. This may be related to the developments in social work practice theory. Professional models of the autonomous worker, the broker, the advocate, all provide paradigms of practice which are useful in intra-campus negotiations.

THE NEW DIALOGUE

A new student life style, characterized by the influence of existential-like theories (however remote) and by strength gained through organization and new identifications, has contributed to a new form of faculty-student dialogue. In the context of the contemporary crisis, previously accepted niceties in human relationships do not retain their traditional acceptance among students and faculty. The new dialogue is different and perhaps more meaningful. Communications stripped of Emily Post-like gentility, at times abrasive, are more often to the point but often, too, contribute toward difficulties in communication. One becomes quickly aware of the restless mood. Also, the style of scholarship in the university is being influenced by the emergence of existentialism. The existential influence on scholarship

62

has been cogently discussed by Dr. James Ackerman. Ackerman comments on the difference between the "existential style" and the "scientific style," noting that the tradition of learning in the American university was based upon the scientific model, now under challenge by many respectable scholars. The existential style challenges the "scientific," organized approach to problem-solving as we have known it.[8]

The new dialogue seems to have obscured sound understandings of communication processes upon which we have relied for many years. We have learned that although students deserve more power in the university, and although most are highly committed to improving the educational system, they may also have blind spots, personal conflicts, "hang-ups" (also true of faculty and administrators). There is sound, social-psychological knowledge that can explain interpersonal behavior. We are aware of it. The tendency not to use it in student negotiations is naive. Communication can break down for this reason—that is, not understanding the social-psychological hang-ups in negotiation or not surfacing those that are understood. Personal needs, face-saving, response to group pressure, loyalty to group principle or class, over-identification with the aggressor, any of these can act as deterrents to effective communication. Part of the responsibility between faculty, students, and administrators for communication is to understand each other's hang-ups and not accept them as inviolate or untouchable. The apparently ever-present concern of students in schools of social work that they may be "psyched out" should be confronted, not avoided.

PAST AND PROLOGUE

We are approaching the end of a five-year period in which there has been conscious effort on the part of social work education as an institution to concern itself with the role of students in decision-making. The Committee on Students (successor to the CSWE Committee on Admissions) of the Council on Social Work Education had its first meeting on December 18, 1967. From then until approximately a year ago the Committee was concerned with ethnic minority students and educationally disadvantaged students rights and responsibilities, in social work education, and policies affecting admissions to schools of social work. As the responsibilities of the committee became more complex, and as it injected itself more forcefully into the student participation scene, the admissions responsibilities were transferred. Later, the Committee on Students transferred its concerns with special needs of minority group students and educationally disadvantaged students to the new special committee on minority groups of the Council. Thus, over this period, the role of students in schools of social work and their participation in decision-making has been gaining attention. There

---

[8]James A. Ackerman, "The Future of the Humanities," *Daedalus, Journal of the American Academy of Arts and Sciences,* Summer, 1969.

was a workshop on student participation at the Deans' Meeting of the Council on Social Work Education Annual Program Meeting in Salt Lake City in January, 1967. This writer presented an exploratory paper at that meeting, raising questions regarding what appeared to be the principal issues in student participation related particularly to curriculum and faculty evaluation. Some of the questions raised were:

1. How much do we know about the extent of student participation in evaluating curricula and faculties in schools of social work?
2. How much do we need to know about the extent and depth of student interest in this area to properly examine its implications?
3. Do *we* want student participation, and why? Do we view student participation as an immediate learning experience for the student or as a contribution to social work education?
4. What should be the limits on student participation and how should they be determined?
5. Are students better equipped to evaluate faculty than they are to evaluate curriculum?
6. What criteria should be used in evaluating faculty and curriculum?
7. How should student evaluations be used?
8. Should faculty participate in the development of evaluative instruments?

The fact that some of these questions are now "academic" is evidence of the progress we apparently have made. However, we don't seem to be any further ahead in answering most of the questions. It is possible that this is because we are still uncomfortable with the *power* implications of student participation and now face additional questions of a different order. Some of these will be discussed below.

In January of 1968, Paul Schreiber, dean of the Hunter College School of Social Work, presented a paper at the Annual Program Meeting entitled: "Student Involvement in Administration and Policy Formulation and in Educational Programs and Curriculum Development."[9] Schreiber pointed out that "historically, precedence can be found for either extreme of an involvement scale if we want to measure the degree of participation. By the second half of the 13th Century, the medieval student universities were participating through their elective representatives and their nations, not only in the election of their own rectors (presidents) but also in the general administration and direction of the entire study process." Schreiber referred to Carlton University, Ottawa, as representing an interesting modern version of a university with a maximum degree of student involvement. "According to information received from (Father) Swithun Bowers, in the coming academic year there will be student representatives on the Senate, on

[9]Paul Schreiber, "Student Involvement in Administration and Policy Formulation and in Educational Programs and Curriculum Development," *Social Work Education Reporter,* Vol. 16, No. 4 (December, 1968), p. 55. Also, *supra,* pp. 31-41.

faculty boards, and on the Faculty Council of the School of Social Work; they will take part in the deliberations and decisions of departments and other bodies responsible for programs of instruction. Student representation on the Board of Governors has also been agreed to in principle." What Schreiber saw as interesting and implied as novel has, in all probability, become close to the norm in most schools of social work today. In a short two years, what appeared to be unique may have become almost commonplace. Information collected by Lilian Ripple in the fall of 1968 reveals the following:

> In 14 schools, student activity related to policy development was through the student organization. Eight schools reported limited or sporadic activity, in spite of some pushing and prodding by deans to get the students to be more active. The situation was very different in the other six schools. There was active student involvement which took the form of student association committees parallel to faculty committees with provision for exchange of ideas, a dean's council, or both.

> The second type of participation was through a joint student-faculty liaison committee, also found in 14 schools. At the time the questionnaires were returned, about half of these schools were considering other forms of committee involvement of students.

> The majority of schools had student members on one or more faculty committees. In almost half of these 44 schools there was a written agreement or guide regarding student members; the 20 with such written statements do not appear to differ in the extent and type of student participation from the 24 whose organizational structure was based upon "general understanding." The number of committees on which students had membership varied greatly, primarily associated with the committee structure in the school. In a few schools, students were members of only one or two committees, usually including the curriculum committee. In general, however, students were members of all committees with the exception of those concerned with faculty appointments, tenure, etc., and to a lesser extent, those concerned with review of student performance.

> Most commonly, there were two or three student members on a committee and students constituted 25 to 40 per cent of the membership. Only eight schools reported any committee with only one student member and this was customary at only two of the 44 schools. Conversely, ten schools reported four or more students on at least some committees.

> In conclusion, the findings of this brief survey show that considerable change has taken place in the policies and practices of graduate schools with respect to students' rights and responsibilities. There is much unevenness and, already, further changes are in process as experience is gained with new patterns. The most immediate need appears to be the development of viable methods of implementation.[10]

---

[10]Lilian Ripple, "Students' Rights and Responsibilities in Graduate Schools of Social Work: Survey of Current Practice," *Social Work Education Reporter,* Vol. 17, No. 2 (June, 1969), p. 48. Also, *supra,* pp. 13-20.

As schools of social work have been developing structures for student participation in decision-making, the institutionalization of student participation has been enhanced by the action of the CSWE. In 1969, on the recommendation of the Committee on Students of the Council, the Board of Directors approved one-third student representation on the Committee on Students, and two students on all standing commissions and committees of the Council, including the Commission on Accreditation. (Every commission and committee of the Council has elected to include students among its membership.)

The Committee on Students also recommended to the Board that the *Manual of Accrediting Standards* be modified so as to protect students' rights and to guarantee them due process in the evaluative process of the school. The *Manual of Accrediting Standards* now includes the new standards on student rights which reads as follows:

> A school should have well-defined and promulgated procedures to protect students against prejudiced or capricious academic evaluations, improper disclosures of students' views, beliefs, and political associations, and limitations upon freedom of expression.
>
> A school's procedures should guarantee students the right to organize in their own interests as students.
>
> A school should establish procedures so that students can contribute to the formulation of institutional policy affecting academic and student affairs.[11]

The National Federation of Student Social Workers is now a constituent member of the CSWE.

Students now sit on the Commission on Accreditation. The Council was the first and probably still the only nationally recognized accrediting association in which students are represented. Within the "establishment agency" of social work education, therefore, the Committee on Students, chaired by Daniel Thurz, is a powerful instrument for student advocacy. It must be admitted that, although the Committee on Students has had an uphill fight in trying to bring about changes which institutionalize student participation, the fight has been encouraged by the Council Board and staff.[12]

I have tried to demonstrate that the role of the students in the decision-making process has been gaining strength during the past four years both in schools of social work and in the Council on Social Work Education. I

---

[11] *Manual of Accrediting Standards* (New York: Council on Social Work Education, 1965, revised 1969), Section 4611.

[12] As one who has been professionally involved in community action in poverty programs, I cannot help but comment on the parallel of this situation with that of the Federal government's encouraging and supporting community action at the neighborhood level. This activity was permitted under Title II-B of the original Economic Opportunity Act of 1964, but for the most part it was removed by administrative fiat after 1965 and later as a result of the Green amendment. The assumption was made before and after these actions that it is in the very nature of the power structure that it cannot nurture dissent. This simply has not been true in the structure of the Committee on Students of the Council on Social Work Education.

have also suggested that the process of involving students in decision-making is in reality a sharing of power within the organizational structure of social work education. Concomitantly, these processes are influenced by the current social revolution in the society, including, significantly, the black revolution and the student revolution.

The issues were identified early by social work educators. These issues continue to present themselves; some remain unsettled. Among those gaining the most attention now are the following:

1. To what extent should student participants be representative of the student body at large, both in particular schools and in the Council on Social Work Education?

This is an external question always raised by students of the democratic process. It was answered during the 18th Century by Edmund Burke in his speech to the electors of Bristol. What Burke said then holds now: There is no way that a representative to a democratic assembly can guarantee that he speaks for a majority of his constituents. To attempt to insure such guarantees is to deny the reality of the democratic process as well as the necessity for some level of efficiency in a very inefficient system. But a second and equally important implication of the question "Whom do you represent?" is that democratically elected representatives in parliamentary bodies (as *students serving* on faculty senates, forums or a variety of faculty committees) do not always represent the majority view on all issues; for the majority view tends usually to be a status quo view and does not usually lend itself to creative change. The majority indeed delegates to its representative the right to speak on its behalf. Burke declared that he would vote his conscience. We should expect nothing less from students.[13]

2. What should be the percentage of student representation on committees? Should they be equal to faculty representation or should they not?

We are still playing the numbers game (both faculties and students). The answer is a political one. Realistically, the amount of student representation will be determined by *what the faculty will accept,* since the faculty now has the power. Arguments about the numbers of student representatives tend to assume that there is a student view and faculty view on issues. This is probably true only in the early stages of student participation in the decision-making process. Students and faculty quickly learn to address themselves to the issues, not to partisan interest. Indeed, partisan interest seems to disappear when faculty and students together address themselves to the business of educational policy making.

3. Directly related to the number of students participating is the ques-

---

[13]"Burke's Speech at the Guildhall in Bristol, 1780," in Edmund Burke, *Works,* Vol. III (London: F. Crivington, 1803), pp. 355-425.

tion as to whether students have the right to be voting members of the committee or participant observers. (In some schools, students still do not have the right to vote.)

It is probably essential that once students are on committees they enjoy the privileges and rights equal to the faculties on the committees. This does not mean to imply, as has been suggested by some, that students are *professionally* equal to faculty. Although this argument of equality seems to be spurious, it is raised often enough to demand a response. Faculty-student professional equality cannot exist since students have not yet achieved a professional status (as we now define "professional"). However, in the task at hand, the analysis of curriculum, for example, or the evalutaion of due process for students, the stake of the students is equal to that of the faculty and their right to participate should be equal. They should, therefore, have the right to vote if the committee arrives at decisions by means of voting.

4. A very important issue deals with the equation between responsibility and authority of students as they attain power in decision-making processes.

Students, if they are to have an equal footing with faculty, have a right to the drudgery of committee work also. Students tend to become intolerant of "nitty-gritty" boring detail of committee work, the endless discussions on what appears to be trivia, or on curriculum theory, or about bibliographies. But, unfortunately, all committee work is not exciting, earthshaking, or even mildly satisfying. In all schools of which I am aware, students are expected to share in all aspects of the committee's work. This is a problem which must be continually examined if student participation is to be seen as a contribution to the academic program and not merely as an instrument for ventilation.

5. The availability of students to participate in school decision-making bodies, given the demands of the academic program, is another issue of high importance.

Committee work is done by students usually over and beyond the requirements of the curriculum, while faculties usually receive credit for committee work as part of their work loads. Even without committee participation, the academic load of students in schools of social work is considerable. As students become increasingly involved in decision-making and there is increasing demand on their time, something will have to give. Some schools have permitted students excused time from field work in order to serve on committees. Some have considered giving credit for participation in committee work. Others have considered making committee work a requirement for all students by rotating committee representation throughout the entire student body on a time-limited basis. What appears repeatedly in discussion about time demands for student participation is the student belief (often reinforced by faculty) that for some courses in the curriculum little is lost if they do not attend. It seems that the dialogue about student participation in decision-making in schools of social work has surfaced a most serious academic problem (one of which we have not been unaware—merely unwilling or unable to accept)—that students are overburdened with a high quantity of low-quality demands. The curricula apparently are not intellectually challenging; they are just heavy in terms of sheer bulk! If student participation is necessary to bring about an upgrading of academic content, let's have more.

6. The question of the authority for making final decisions has been raised repeatedly.

Schreiber, in the article already cited, said "a quality, however, inherent in administration is that it carries final responsibility and accountability usually to the President and/or the Board of Trustees of the University. It is the place where 'the buck stops' and cannot be 'passed' any further. Corollary to this responsibility must be the right and authority to make a final decision. This does not mean arbitrary or unilateral authoritarianism but, on the contrary, careful consideration of various interests and viewpoints of arguments from all sides and of varying alternatives but ultimately the administrator must make his own decisions."[14]

Five years of discussions with students about their role in decision-making in the Adelphi School of Social Work, as well as my experience as a member of the Committee on Students in the Council, has never once revealed any challenge on the part of the students to the right of ultimate authority on the part of the faculty and administration. The shared power issue for social work students has to do with the right to participate here and now. Philosophical or fundamental debate is regarded by the students as a subterfuge on the part of faculty or administration to avoid dealing with present reality.

SUMMARY

This paper has concerned itself with the dimensions of power-sharing as participation of students in decision-making in schools of social work increases. The posture of social work education for the most part has been accepting, not to all student demands, but of the principle of power-sharing. Although all the results are not and will not be in for years to come, comments from individual deans, committee chairmen, and other faculty members suggest that the yielding posture and the consequent sharing of power has resulted in a more satisfying process of decision-making for faculty as well as students. Also, it has resulted in changes in curriculum, program and administrative structures in many schools of social work.

---

[14]Schreiber, *op. cit.*, p. 57.

Regardless of the desirable posture of social work education in its efforts to realign the processes for decision-making, the fact is that students seem willing to risk a great deal, indeed their own education, in the interest of a better educational system. Not to yield to the principle of shared power, and not to become engaged in a serious and committed effort to redefine systems of educational control, is to opt for an educational system controlled by an educational elite. But knowing that academic knowledge does not bestow academic infallibility and being aware that the world is in revolution and that all authority systems are being redefined, we are left, sadly or gladly, (depending on your bias), but realistically, with very little choice.

FACULTY, STUDENTS, ADMINISTRATION, AND DECISION MAKING: AN EXPERIENCE IN INTERDEPENDENCE

PHYLLIS CAROFF
and
LILLIAN C. LAMPKIN

REPORTED IN THIS PAPER are the perceptions and the evolution of a position of two faculty members of the Hunter College School of Social Work who have been intimately involved in the school's attempts to achieve a maximally functional design for student participation in decision making. We are sure we will find consensus in the assumption that any plan for governance must be viable in terms of the life of the institution. Ideally, such plans grow out of rational processes that recognize the intrinsic mutual interdependence of the various constitutencies in the school community. In the process of developing a position, we perceive that where we are at this moment in time reflects the influence of conceptualizations that have appeared in the literature,[1] validated at least in part and for the present by the Hunter experience.

Our conception assumes that there is a contract between the university and the student in a professional school which establishes certain constraints differing from the undergraduate situation by virtue of the nature of professional education. In a professional school, there is the expectation that students will acquire knowledge that will be integrated with values in order to develop skill in the responsible delivery of service. It is also expected that the graduate social work student is a relatively mature individ-

---

[1] See, for example: Paul Schreiber, "Student Involvement in Administration and Policy Formulation and in Educational Programs and Curriculum Development," *Social Work Education Reporter,* Vol. 16, No. 4 (December, 1968), p. 55, and, *supra,* pp. 31-41; Winifred Bell, "Educational Bases for Student Involvement in the Administration of Social Work Schools," *Social Work Education Reporter,* Vol. 17, No. 4 (December, 1969), pp. 56-59, and *supra,* pp. 41-49; Amitai Etzioni, "Confessions of a Professor Caught in a Revolution," *The New York Times Magazine,* September 15, 1968; *Rights and Responsibilities: The University Dilemma, Daedalus,* Summer, 1970, especially Walter P. Metzger, "The Crisis of Academic Authority;" and Joseph Vigilante, "Student Participation in Decision-Making in Schools of Social Work," *Journal of Education for Social Work,* Vol. 6, No. 2 (Fall, 1970), and *supra,* pp. 57-71.

ual who has successfully completed four years of undergraduate education and has had prior experience predisposing him to the choice of social work as a profession. Moreover, implicit in the selection of students is the assumption (right or wrong) that they have already achieved a value system not too disparate from that held by the profession. This value system implies that there are commonly held goals between faculty and students about the necessity to meet human need. This commonality of goals should, in a measure, accommodate some of the tension intrinsic to the differential statuses and roles of faculty and students.

In contrast to values and primary goals, however, the expertise of knowledge and skill evolves out of cumulative learning and experience. It is this expertise, a requirement of faculty, which confers on them the competence and responsibility to ensure a curriculum from which students will achieve practice skills that will be functional in a changing society.

In looking back on our experience during the period of confrontation,[2] we are impressed with the extent to which faculty decisions were reactive to pressure and highly political. Although we recognize that politics is a part of the human condition, responsible power-sharing requires accountability and the integration of change with continuity. At times we resist change, not simply from an unwillingness to share power, but out of a real concern for the continuity and viability of the educational process. On other occasions, we concede radical changes that have not been carefully thought through.

For some time the changing climate in our school had legitimized student participation in evaluation of course content and curriculum development. Two students were voting members of the curriculum committee. Their suggestions and criticisms had helped to quicken the pace of curriculum modification. In addition, each class as a group had utilized its own process to deal with differences of opinion, needs for innovation, and, for the most part, arrived at considered recommendations. Thus, student materials were used more readily; bibliographies were expanded and updated. In many ways, a major enrichment of the curriculum resulted.

In response to student confrontation, however, prior sequence structures were reorganized to provide for student representatives from each class to participate with faculty in reworking specific curriculum content. In some sequences student representatives outnumbered faculty on these committees. In response to groups of students most articulate about their special interest, courses were proliferated. A series of alternatives to theses as a means of fulfilling research requirements were established.

When committees addressed the implementation of curriculum decisions

---

[2]In the spring semester, 1969, a group of students boycotted classes in protest against the non-reappointment of a faculty member. This event became the catalyst for the expression of long-standing strains related to both administrative and curricular problems. Subsequently, a majority of the students voted to support their colleagues in this action, which resulted in a boycott of all classes for six weeks.

—selection and preparation of teaching material—student participation proved dysfunctional. Student unavailability and lack of expertise precluded the accomplishment of necessary tasks. Whether this is a question of motivation, competence, or just simply time remains unanswered. However, the larger question is whether the participation of students in the implementation process is appropriate. If our assumptions about expertise are valid, then it is the responsibility of the faculty to do whatever is necessary to carry out the intent of curriculum. Based on the cumulative learning, the sense of continuity, and the responsibility, it is the faculty who must perform the essential tasks as their part of the educational contract. In our conception, students make their contributions through feedback and evaluation in the classroom, which we see as a necessary process.

Moreover, with respect to curriculum policy and planning, we believe that students have both a contribution and appropriate responsibility. The issue is how to develop ways to maximize student input and minimize the problems related to competence for those students interested in such participation. Much work is needed to bring student participation in this area to the level which assures acceptance of students as full participants in the process. Furthermore, it needs to be recognized that the most interested and articulate students do not necessarily represent the majority of student thinking. This raises a question of accountability. In our school, we experienced a tension between the most interested, frequently most able, and the need for students to be accountable to their larger constituency. For all of these reasons we believe that to preserve viability and continuity in curriculum planning, a balance in favor of faculty representation is required. In the recent period of greater calm, we observe that many students recognizing their loss in the confrontation have "returned to the books" and are dissatisfied with those changes which are reactive. Made politically, without the opportunity for reflection and integration, such changes are no more relevant than the prior approaches which they superseded.

In retrospect, it would appear that student governance had been used as an all-inclusive rubric. As we now attempt to analyze our school's experience, we believe there are three levels of decision making subsumed under the notion of governance: long-range planning, intermediate policy, and implementation. Long-range planning, the determination of educational thrusts, and the unique mission of the school—a determination which is value-based—provide the opportunity for student input, and such input is essential here. Values, unlike knowledge and skill, are not cumulative and should inform the directions and emphasis of curriculum planning. In our rapidly changing society, both students and faculty face many ambiguities. In many ways students, because they are on the firing line, perceive these ambiguities; many faculty do not. Therefore, feedback from student experience must be considered in long-range decisions.

The "mission" of the school has its implications for the intermediate level of policy making. Included in this level are decisions about aspects of admissions, financial aid, and course objectives. For example, in the admissions process, decisions must be made about whether and to what degree the student population will reflect the composition of the community in which the school is located. The extent to which the school will invest its resources in providing the supports necessary to accept students considered educationally at risk is another policy decision at this level. Similar illustrations can be developed in the area of financial aid and the objectives for any individual course. Insofar as this level of policy making reflects the long-range thrusts of the institution and in turn may influence such planning, here, too, students should have representation.

However, when we move to determining which particular applicant will be accepted, we are at the level of implementation. Similarly, when we look at the day-to-day decisions about course content and its organization in sequence, we come to the implementing tasks of faculty and administrative personnel requiring specific expertise, continuity, and accountability. As indicated above, our experience would suggest that student participation in decision making at this level is non-viable.

However, the one area of implementation in which student participation has been maximally effective has been on those committees dealing with student status. Student review procedures negotiated out of the first major confrontation at Hunter have proved to be workable. Structures for review evolved out of a struggle for power sharing, and the "numbers game" was an inevitable and significant factor in determining committee composition. The students insisted in the negotiations on a significant percentage of representation (50 percent) to guarantee their rights and due process. However, they accepted that in those committees having final decision-making powers, there should be a larger number of faculty (including administration)—a ratio of three to two.

Our experience bears out the observation that once the struggle seems to be resolved, the committees in truth functioned as school committees, and differences did not reflect the vested interest of either constituency. The students' recognition of the importance of the committee's charge was reflected in their choice of representatives. The more articulate and activist students who led the struggle for change were not necessarily those chosen as student representatives. After two years, with minor procedural modifications, these processes are evaluated positively by students, faculty, and administration.

At this juncture it is important to consider the question of faculty evaluation. We believe in the importance of student feedback on faculty presentation of content and the responsiveness of faculty to students as well as the students' overall reactions to a course. This feedback has been formalized in an evaluation process, the content of which is available to the individual faculty member and administration. These evaluations are seriously considered in decisions about reappointment and tenure. However, the question remains as to whether students should participate in personnel decisions. In the final analysis, the ultimate decisions about personnel must be made by the institution in the light of its overall needs, with cumulative student feedback incorporated in the process. At the City University of New York this process begins with student and peer evaluation and proceeds through channels to the Board of Higher Education, which has the final institutional responsibility.

So far, we have been considering that part of the educational process that is essentially "on campus." We recognize that the field raises similar questions and poses many unresolved issues. At Hunter, changes in curriculum and student review procedures evolved out of confrontation and negotiations between constituencies of the campus community, yet field instructors are invited, even required, to participate in the review process. Moreover, increasing demands are being made by students and faculty for broadening and enriching the field experience. Increasingly, students participate in the placement process and evaluate the overall field experience as well as their field instruction. However, the ultimate decision regarding field placement and personnel relies upon the mission of the school—about which students have a say—available resources, and educational assessment. Here again, faculty with administrative sanction has final decision-making responsibility.

SUMMARY

At Hunter, we have found that when students experience the curriculum as facilitating their goal of learning how to help people, the politics of governance assume a lesser proportion. Most view their participation in policy making primarily within the frame of reference of the educational experience. The struggle for power more often than not has reflected dissatisfaction with content and a lack of responsiveness on the part of faculty to changing needs. This is not to ascribe malevolence to faculty but to reflect some of the strains in system maintenance vis-a-vis the need for flexibility. Unquestionably, the student struggle for change has infused the curriculum with vitality.

The question is how to sustain a core program on the one hand, while on the other to evaluate periodically both structure and content in order to determine that the program carries out the common goals of both student and faculty. We cannot expect that the student press for change can take into account the strain between their urgent demand to meet need and the orderly process of learning which is part and parcel of the theoretical underpinnings informing practice. It is the responsibility of the faculty to maintain this perspective. Faculty must fulfill its responsibility for so do-

75

ing by relating to the practice issues with which students are confronted. Implicit in this is the need for structures enabling faculty to maintain the necessary awareness of the issues and the conflicts which the profession confronts.

At this point, students and administration in our school have accepted and are in the process of implementing a school Senate that incorporates the previously negotiated procedures of student review and excludes structures mandated by the University.[3]

The events leading to this have moved us toward clarifying differential roles of administration, faculty, and students vis-a-vis the School of Social Work and Hunter College. We no longer are a small school, functioning as an "academy of peers" and unclear about the differential rights and responsibilities of faculty, students, and administration. Out of the struggle with students we have moved toward greater clarification of *who* has responsibility for *what* and to *whom*. This has helped to articulate rewards and sanctions inherent in the university system.

More than ever, there is the need for reason to prevail. In any process of change, decisions have to be made about the viability and consequences of new structures and procedures as they impinge on the survival and growth of the institution. In our concept, there can be no hardening of the lines between constituencies. There is an interdependence between the university and its students which is essential to the life of the organization and the goals of the students. This becomes increasingly clear as the anti-professional forces appear to be moving in ways which undercut mutually held values in the profession.

---

[3]See: Personnel & Budget Committee, Section 8, 10, *Bylaws of Board Higher Education* February, 1971 (revised), New York, N.Y. Board of Higher Education.

STUDENT INVOLVEMENT IN THE GOVERNANCE OF SCHOOLS OF SOCIAL WORK: IMPLICATIONS FOR SOCIAL WORK EDUCATION AND PRACTICE*

EDWARD ALAN SWANSON

THE CURRENT TREND in education is participation of students in administrative and policy formulating committees. In general, this has taken the form of a representative democracy; namely, a certain number or proportion of students are on various committees and boards. In some cases the debate is whether students should be allowed to participate at all, and in others the debate centers around what percentage of any one committee or board should be students.

Before getting into the specifics of graduate schools of social work, let us look, in a general way, at the recent trend toward student participation in the governance of universities. On the one hand there is question about the learning experience itself. Colleges and universities have become large bureaucratic institutions not unlike the telephone company, the Internal Revenue Service, the selective service board, etc., and in such bureaucracies there is a tendency to routinize and compartmentalize by areas of expertise, which in turn leads to an impersonal structure. In these institutions, the individual must adapt to the system and not the system to the individual. This impersonalization, Paul Goodmen suggests, creates discontents for all actors in the system. He writes:

> The present expanded school systems are coercive in their nature. The young have to attend for various well known reasons, none of which is necessary for their well-being or the well-being of society. Then when a small militant group defies the coercive institution and shouts 'Shut it down', the majority are cooly complacent because they don't care for the place either. And since the catchall expansion makes serious academic work impossible, many of the faculty are complacent about the shutdown too.[1]

[1] Paul Goodman, "High School Is Too Much," *Psychology Today,* Vol. 4, No. 5 (October, 1970), p. 25.

*This paper was originally presented at the Eighteenth Annual Program Meeting of the Council on Social Work Education in Seattle, Washington, January 27, 1971.

The student soon learns that he is at college to be processed. His goal often becomes how to get through rather than learning in itself. Cramming, memorizing, and plagiarizing are often what are rewarded. Because students are unhappy with their experience, they are demanding a voice in such matters as curriculum change, faculty appointments and retention, a revision of the grading system, and other related areas in which they feel changes are needed.

Related to the learning experience itself, but somewhat different, is the role of the university as it relates to society as a whole. The student, among others, is constantly bombarded with the numerous issues facing us as a society: poverty, racism, pollution, war, drug abuse, etc. (Indeed, many students go into the field of social work with the expectation of effecting some change in these or other areas.)

The university not only seems to lag behind in addressing itself to these problems, but in many instances it is contributing to them. Those faculty and administrators who appeal to the "neutrality" of the university are fooling fewer and fewer people.

It seems the universities have in many ways accepted the priorities of the government and industry without seriously looking at the ethics associated with those priorities. The universities have often accepted a marketplace morality. As a case in point, when the physics professor accepts a government contract to do war-related research under the auspices of the university, the university cannot claim such neutrality. The field of science has generally claimed ethical neutrality and has disseminated knowledge that is void of any code of ethics as a consequence. Many students seriously doubt that science and scientists can continue to claim such neutrality and are particularly concerned that the university has attempted to do so. The neutral role of the university in its relationship to society is questionable to many students in light of the university involvement in military research, military training through R.O.T.C., monetary investments in racist or military-related corporations, engagement in intercollegiate athletics with racist institutions, and so the list goes.

With this brief backdrop, I think it is quite evident why students should get involved with the governing of the university, and, indeed, why they have. Students in some areas are causing or have caused some anxiety to administrators and faculty. The response, with much debate, has been to allow students more and more involvement in various committees. I say "with much debate" because there is still some resistance to allowing students on administrative committees. In terms of schools of social work, the issue generally seems to be the proportion of student representation rather than whether or not students should be represented.

Many proposals allowing for various ratios of student-faculty representation have been offered and some have been implemented. The School of Social Work at the University of Michigan uses a method which is viewed by most there as a "good balance." All committees have 50 per cent students and 50 per cent faculty, with the chairman of each committee being a faculty member. In cases of a tie vote, the chairman casts the deciding vote.[2] A variety of plans could be catalogued but that is not the issue I wish to deal with at this time. I am concerned with how students most effectively bring about change, change that reflects our interests and our concerns.

I doubt that, at this point in time, the most effective means for social work students to effect change within their schools is by directing all their energy into student-faculty committees. I say this for several reasons. First, schools of social work are bureaucratic structures in themselves and very much a part of an even larger bureaucracy; the inertia to change is formidable. As members of committees, students tend to start looking at change as innately slow as they, too, realize the vast maize through which change is transmitted. Making changes often requires the understanding and approval of many different individuals and groups. Each step in the process seems reasonable, and when students are intimately involved they begin to see the step-by-step reasoning in the process and to accept it. It's amazing, however, how quickly those steps melt away when there's a crisis. Our curricular committee at the University of Washington had been meeting for three years to come up with a new curricular design for the School of Social Work, and yet, during a recent student strike, within one week the faculty accepted a drastic revision in curriculum for the remainder of the year.

Second, I see a real danger in students thinking that participation with faculty and administration will necessarily bring about change. If anything, it may lead to more bureaucracy than already exists, and time is on the side of faculty and administration. Meetings can be tedious and unproductive unless there is a certain commitment to movement.

Third, as students we have different methods of effecting change than either faculty or administration, and we need to develop and use those methods. The faculty and administration are bound to the collegial system, whereas we are not. Often students view faculty as a monolithic body, without whose approval little or no change can occur. Many times the faculty and administration are as trapped by the system as the students. As Joseph Lyford points out:

> Anybody who has ever dealt with a government bureaucracy knows that there is an enormous difference between the views held by the individuals who run it and what the bureaucracy as an institution does despite the wishes of everybody in it. And here, once more, the old liberal presumption that we are a society based upon participational democratic procedures has turned out to be an illusion.[3]

---

[2]John L. Erlich and John E. Tropman, "The Politics of Participation: Student Power," *Social Work*, Vol. 14, No. 4 (October, 1969), pp. 70-71.

[3]Joseph P. Lyford, "The Establishment and All That," *The Establishment and All That* (Santa Barbara, California: The Center for the Study of Democratic Insitutions, 1970), pp. 24-25.

Lyford also relates a conversation he had with a professor friend during the disturbance at Columbia University over building the gymnasium in Morningride Park. His friend said:

> We've got to recognize that in doing this to Columbia at least the students are giving us a chance to get in there and do things about this University that have needed to be done for a long time.[4]

Many times our goals are the same, but our methods are different. The following is an example of such an instance. At the school of social work of one university, the students and faculty met in committees on the issue of minority recruitment and financial aid to minority students; this was an issue on which both faculty and students essentially agreed. Through the dean, a proposal was submitted to the university-at-large. Time elapsed and nothing happened. Finally, after frequent prodding, the dean was able to get a response from the university-at-large which said that they, too, were in agreement with the proposal, but that there were no funds available. At that point, a half-dozen Black and Asian students formed a group, obtained support from the Black Student Union and the Asian Coalition as well as some other community groups, and met with the dean on the rejected proposal. Within a month money had been allocated for the implementation of the proposal.

The above example can also be used to begin discussion of methods for effecting change available to students. In the above example, the main difference between the group that went through 'normal channels' and the *ad hoc* group was that the *ad hoc* groups used the implicit threat of conflict. Unfortunately, indications are that for at least short-term change to occur, there has to be a relatively high level of anxiety. And students are finding that collectively they can produce that anxiety through conflict.

Conflict often carries with it a negative connotation. It's disruptive, ungentlemanly, anxiety-producing, and shows bad faith, yet at the same time it has been one of the most useful tools for democracy. The labor movement would never have accomplished wage increases or improved working conditions by presenting logical arguments in a gentlemenly way and occasionally appealing to the moral responsibilities of management. It took conflict. In their struggle the Blacks have found that conflict is generally necessary in order to realize any semblance of democracy. Democracy in terms of voting wasn't realized by women until they resorted to conflict. To be sure, conflict, like any tool, can be used to build or destroy. We as students—and more specifically, as social work students—need to learn how to use conflict in a constructive way if democracy is to be realized for us.

There are many other methods that might be more useful to students than expending all their energies in student-faculty committees. One meth-

---

[4]*Ibid.*, p. 27.

od might be to set up a parallel committee structure. Many functions performed by faculty committees are routine and maintenance-oriented. In parallel committees, not only can the students deal with issues directly affecting students, but strategies and tactics can be worked out. The involvement of recent alumni, community groups, or other student groups can often be an asset. The earlier example indicated the effectiveness of involving the Black Student Union and Asian Coalition around the issue of minority recruitment.

Often an *ad hoc* group can be used as a substitute for an existing committee, particularly when an issue emerges that needs immediate attention. There are certain advantages to *ad hoc* groups. Students can concentrate on one particular issue and, rather than going through existing structures, can often deal directly with the people involved. These groups can be small and work on the persuasion of certain faculty and administrators, or they can be large and highly organized and directed toward the university-at-large.

Certainly an important method available to us is student participation on faculty and administrative committees. Students should be part of faculty committees, but it seems that the primary concern of students should be to effect policy and see to it that that policy is implemented. If it becomes necessary to accomplish that by increasing student representation on any one particular committee, then that should be the strategy. Student participation should be just one of a range of methods used, not the sole method or perhaps worse, the method that's looked at as an end in itself.

Before looking at some of the issues about which students are concerned, it is necessary to look at the students themselves. To classify or suggest that many social work students are revolutionaries is a mistake. I cannot imagine a commited revolutionary coming to a school of social work for training. Indeed, the student who does come to graduate school usually has had some experience in the field of social work and has been selected as a student for graduate training based on intellectual ability, maturity, ability to deal with stress, and potential to be an effective change agent.

In general, the student's life experiences and educational experiences have been different from those of the faculty. By that, I mean that our experiences have come from a different time and place, and, because of this, our perceptions are often different. The student's perceptions are his, however, and they are real, and the faculties' are theirs and they are real. The faculty and students both ought to accept that rationally.

The issues on which students want a say are many and varied. In the area of curriculum there are a whole host of issues. One of the important yet more difficult to deal with is individualization of the student. The 'empty basket' theory—the assumption that every student comes as an empty vessel to be filled at the fountain of social work education—that seems to be part of many schools of social work is both insulting and inefficient. This gives no credit to the student's previous life experience or future expectations.

Many students want more emphasis on changing existing institutions rather than training in how to be part of them. This applies to both classroom experiences as well as field experience, perhaps with the idea of integrating the two with a view toward change. Wineman and James point out the dichotomy that often exists between class and field.

> Students go into these (field) settings every year—like so many ants marching out of the hill—all with their shiny new theory and methods gear in their little knapsacks, ready to 'help.' (None of them was ever born that naive, but that's the pretend game they and the faculty play.) They are systematically taught to abandon reality. . . . When the student expresses these concerns, the faculty more or less falls back on avoidance responses, which can only be characterized as a system of defense against change.[5]

Certainly there are other needed curriculum changes and they vary from school to school.

Another area that students are concerned about is faculty hiring and retention. The faculty member is supposedly chosen because of his proven ability, intellectual capacity, and commitment and desire to keep abreast of the rapidly expanding body of knowledge in his particular area of expertise. Most students are aware of some faculty members whose lectures and bibliographies can be used to date their entry to the faculty.

Due process for students is also needed in many schools. 'Counseling out' can be a very effective means on the part of faculty and administration to stifle dissent by the elimination of dissident students.

In terms of students effecting the complexion of social work and social work education, probably the most important area for students to work on is admission and scholarships. With most schools of social work receiving far more applications than they have openings, the complexion of the student body can be drastically modified by the choice of who is admitted and who gets scholarships.

The list could go on in terms of specific issues that relate in differing importance to various schools, but the important point is that if students are to become a real part in the governance of their schools and are to make an impact on social work and social work education, it's going to take more than representative democracy.

This discussion of the student as change agent within the school of social work does have implications for the social worker as change agent in practice. It implies a shift in the methods that many social workers traditionally have used.

First, getting into the system to bring about change from within is not enough. Working directly within the system, in a participatory sense, does

---

[5]David Wineman and Adrienne James, "The Advocacy Challenge to Schools of Social Work," *Social Work*, Vol. 14, No. 2 (April, 1969), pp. 26-27.

not seem to be the most effective means of effecting change. The goals of the worker and many of those in a particular agency or institution may be essentially the same, but somehow change seems slow in coming. Rather than just working within the institution, there seems to be some merit in working from outside at the same time. An example of this is a social workers' union, made up of employees in a welfare department. Within the structure of the union they can set up committees or action groups centered around the same issues that the department has to deal with but from a different perspective and a different stance. Even if the department has an enlightened administration, they cannot use the same strategies and tactics as the union (or any other organized group of social workers, for that matter).

Second, conflict should not be looked at as unprofessional, undemocratic, or anti-intellectual, but rather as potentially a useful tool for effecting change. This may require a change in stance of many social workers but certainly not in social work values.

Perhaps the largest implication for social work practice is that students are in many and various ways demanding changes in social work as it is taught and as it is practiced. Fewer and fewer students want to be junior therapists who unobtrusively fit into an institution. More and more students expect to learn how to change institutions and are finding that they have to start with the school of social work itself.

STUDENT PARTICIPATION
IN DECISION MAKING
IN HIGHER EDUCATION

THE POLITICS
OF ACADEMIA

KINGMAN BREWSTER, JR.

IN MY REPORT for the academic year 1968-69 I stated the considerations which seemed to me to bear on any consideration of a university's "governance" and I ventured a few very general propositions. Nothing that has happened here or elsewhere in the intervening year has caused me to change my mind. Last year's experience at Yale and on other campuses, however, has stimulated more thought about how to make the work and direction of the university more responsive to the needs and interests of all its members.

The main thrust of most current reappraisals and proposals concerning how a university should be run have supposed that there should be a broader and more "democratic" participation by students in the decisions of the faculty. They also seek a broader and more democratic participation by both faculty and students in decisions traditionally reserved to the administration and trustees. The central issue in the ensuing debate has been how far this participation should be broadened, and how democratic the selection of participants should be. This certainly has been the focus of the discussion at Yale, both last spring by various student groups and unofficial "open" meetings and during the summer in the deliberations of an ad hoc group of faculty and students who were asked to act as an advisory committee to Mr. Jorge Dominguez. Mr. Dominguez, a Yale College graduate of the class of 1967, currently a Junior Fellow and candidate for the Ph.D. in Government at Harvard University, was asked by me to review the proposals and developments at other institutions and to recommend how Yale might best constitute a "legitimate" group of faculty, students, and others to make formal recommendations for the improvement of Yale's "governance."

In past reports, speeches, and conversations I have encouraged more avenues for student participation. But I have also pecked skeptically at the notion of institutionalized representation as the cure-all for discontent, or

Reprinted with permission of the author from Thoughts on University Government *(New Haven, Connecticut: Yale University, 1969), pp. 19-28.*

87

as the principal prescription for improvement. Taking an advocate's aim at a straw man when he sees one, I have blasted the extreme and extremely silly notion that "pure" one-man-one-vote democracy would best determine the work and direction of a university. Although this opportunity was afforded by questions seriously put by an undergraduate editor, it is doubtful whether even he would have answered his own questions affirmatively.

Even if we could knock most radical participatory democrats and most reactionary traditional autocrats off their extreme perches, however, there does remain a fundamental choice of emphasis which must be made, and which is really receiving almost no attention at all. I have done no more than hint at it timidly in the past because I was not sure where I came out. Now I am. I am convinced that *representation* is not the clue to university improvement. Indeed, if carried too far it could lead to disaster. I am, rather, now convinced that *accountability* is what we should be striving for.

Champions of representation of students to vote in all groups, committees, boards, and meetings make the appealing point that a student should be able to participate in the decisions which affect him.

Now, obviously his opinion should be taken into consideration, just as his interests should be taken into account. But the current mood is that he should be able to have a large say in actually making the final decisions on all matters. "Power-sharing" is the cry.

On some matters I have indicated before that the self-determination of the faculty, collective academic freedom from the pressure to please or the fear of displeasure, requires that the faculty be able to meet in camera on issues of appointments, degree standards, and the recommendation of degrees. But leaving these sanctuaries aside, there is the very real question of whether it is in the best interest of the students themselves not only to make their voices heard but to try to govern the place. Put differently, it is pertinent to ask, "will the place be better or worse in terms of the student's own interest in the quality of his education if the responsibility for its direction is assumed by student representatives or if it resides primarily with the faculty and administration?"

The answer to this question depends upon your assumptions not only about the relative wisdom of students in general and the wisdom of established faculty and administrative authorities. It also depends upon how truly representative you think student governors would be.

I happen to think that in a world in which ideas and policies and institutions have a high rate of obsolescence, the young are more perceptive on many matters, wiser if you will, than their elders. On the other hand, experience has its claim. And in a self-perpetuating institution the claims of continuity have to be weighed against the claims of "now."

Judgments can differ about this. But whatever they are, I am moved by another very practical consideration, on the basis of admittedly short experience and inadequate sample. I do not think that the great *majority* of students want to spend *very much* of their time or energy in the guidance and governance of their university. They want to live and learn up to the hilt, and make the most of what they know to be a very unusual and remarkably short opportunity to develop their capacities by trial and error in the pursuit of personal enthusiasms. Over and over again this has been demonstrated even in times of crises which shook and threatened the existence of the institution. In the longer, duller life between crises it is even more demonstrable that to the average student the purpose of university life is learning and living, not governing. The long and unimpressive history of "sand box" student government is fair warning that student politics, like the politics of professional associations (ABA, AMA, etc.), cannot be counted on always to draw out the most talented members of the constituency or to capture the attention and concern, day in and day out, of the eligible voters.

These misgivings have nothing to do with either skepticism of the motivation or scorn for the competence of those students who may be actively interested in university government. In fact, their zeal is good for the university and a chance to participate is good for them. At best, however, they are a minority.

From time to time the opportunity for spokesmanship in the name of student opinion will be seized by a wholly unrepresentative group. This may be by election, by the domination of open meetings, or simply by outlasting others who are less single-minded in their political interest.

Two assumptions led me to the conviction that broader sharing of responsibility for ultimate academic decisions is not the primary thrust of useful university reform. The first is: *the majority is not sufficiently interested in devoting their time and attention to the running of the university to make it likely that "participatory democracy" will be truly democratic.*

The second is: *most students would rather have the policies of the university directed by the faculty and administration than by their classmates.* This is pure speculation. The question has never been thus bluntly put. The only reason I come to this conclusion, I suppose, is because I would feel that way. I would insist on a right not only to be heard but listened to. But I would think that the institution would do a better job and be more likely to make bold decisions swiftly and decisively if ultimate responsibility for its direction were sharply focused on the shoulders of people who are devoting their personal energies and risking their professional reputations, full-time, for the best years of their lives, for the quality of the institution— whether as committeemen, department chairmen, deans, officers, provosts, or presidents.

Not only the capacity to make decisions boldly and consistently but the quality of those decisions urge that inherently executive matters not be distorted by being poured into a quasi-legislative process in the name of representation. If the allocation of resources is put into a legislative process, it can only devolve into a log-rolling, pork-barrel exercise with each interest group trying to take more and give less. The search for outside support cannot be dictated by any detailed, legislated directive or control; needs must be matched to opportunities. The prospect of getting twice as much for the lesser need must be weighed against the chance of getting much less or nothing at all if other priorities are stubbornly insisted upon with all potential donors. As in all negotiation, individual conviction and intuition has to be relied upon. The delays and embarrassments of public discussion of particular approaches for outside support would chill the market and rob the executive of its ability to speak with the confidence and conviction which is the essence of "selling" the institution to potential supporters—public or private. Finally, there is an intangible element of character and personality on which any donor must rely when he puts his funds in trust. This would be diluted if the donor felt that the destiny of his gift depended on the rise and fall of political fortunes in a representative assembly whose members he could not possibly come to know with the intimacy which inspires confidence.

I am now convinced that the political symbolism of participatory democracy is an illusion when applied to many of the academic and financial decisions which direct an academic institution; and that the slogans of representative democracy could lead to even greater misrepresentation of the student's interest in the quality of his institution if they implied the sharing of the faculty's academic responsibility. Either one, if carried to ultimate legislative supremacy, could stultify the capacity to steer the place boldly and decisively in times that require imagination and rapid change.

The answer to the legitimate student demand for great *individual* self-determination is wider and wider latitude for academic as well as personal choice, including the choice of whether and when to stay at the institution, now inhibited by an outrageous selective service system.

The answer to the legitimate student demand to have protection against incompetent and unresponsive administration is not formal *representation* in all matters. It is administrative *accountability*.

I would urge radical reform to make real the promise of administrative accountability precisely because I am skeptical of the reality of either participatory or representative democracy as a way of making final university decisions.

The first requirement of accountability is disclosure. Those affected by policies and decisions cannot hold those who make them to account unless there is full and adequate public access to the record of the process by which the decision was made. Reasons of good manners or simple humanity may make it desirable from time to time to impose a seal of confidence on one man's opinion about another, in the admissions or appointment processes in particular. Unless opinion can be received in confidence in

90

ach cases, it well may be withheld or watered down to banalities in order to avoid offense or injury.

There also may be situations where the intentions of the institution in its dealing with adversary outside interests make it very unwise to tip one's hand by public disclosure. In an impending real estate deal there is no reason why the university should be deprived of its bargaining power by having to reveal the inner thoughts about what the outside price would be. In a legal proceeding there is no reason why the university should forfeit its right to devise its strategy in confidential talks with counsel and others involved.

But these are exceptions which can be reserved for executive sessions and confidential minutes. Hiatus could be noted in the record, specifying the nature of the problem and the reasons for exceptional confidentiality. Otherwise, it seems to me that the record should be public. At the very least, there should be a public communique. It might be even better if there were literal transcripts. Even if such transcripts were rarely resorted to, their availability would be the best assurance that the university could not be governed by conspiracy and that the reasons given by way of explanation were in fact the reasons for decision. Obviously the self-consciousness which this would impose might be an inhibition. It certainly will be opposed by traditionalists who value the men's club atmosphere of confidential deliberation. Some form of convincing access to the record of proceedings and the reason for decision seems to me far, far preferable to the widening and diluting of the responsibility for decisions. If accountability as an alternative to representation is to be convincing, disclosure must be as nearly complete as possible.

The second requirement of accountability is the right of petition by those affected by decisions. There has to be a legitimate, easy, and reliable way in which critical opinion can be generated and communicated. Informal access through a variety of channels is the best way to do this in a relatively healthy situation. But if lack of confidence in authority spreads to a numerically significant minority of any of the constituent parts of the university—students or faculty (or alumni, for that matter)—then there should be an understood channel of petition to whatever level is responsible for the appointment to the post or office whose conduct is the subject of complaint.

If a large majority most of the time, or a significant minority all of the time, is willing to delegate the job of policy-making and direction to faculty and administrative leadership, it is especially important to be sure that when this confidence is lost something can be done about it through legitimate channels. Accountability as a substitute for representation presupposes that those who are entrusted with responsibility will feel the hot breath of accountability day in and day out. This will be so only if petition can reach and gain response from those in a position to act, at a level above those complained of.

The third essential element, if accountability is to be real, is some regular, understood process whereby reappraisal of the competence of administration and the community's confidence in it can be undertaken without waiting for a putsch or rebellion.

At Yale this takes place pretty regularly in the case of college masters, department chairmen, and deans. Unlike many universities, every administrative appointment is for a term of years; three for chairmen, five for masters and deans. Naturally there is a presumption in favor of renewal if the man is willing. But after a second term there is generally an expectation that the man will revert to his purely academic status as a teacher and scholar.

This expectation of impermanent administrative appointment has many obvious virtues. It passes around the burdens of academic administration so that over the cycle of a generation more points of view are brought to bear, more people are involved and see the institution from the vantage point of important responsibility. Hardening of the academic arteries is less likely to set in. Most important of all, the relatively short term assures both the institution and the man that there is an honorable and humane discharge which does not imply dissatisfaction on either side. Given this opportunity for periodic reappraisal, the President is in a position to solicit and react constructively to criticisms and malaise without waiting for the mobilization of malcontentment in the form of petition. Recent experience with the appointment of new masters and new deans has shown that a little time and trouble can bring to bear on such appointments the authentic views of the students and faculty affected. This should be no less true when the issue is renewal of an existing appointment, and any self-respecting, self-confident dean would welcome it.

But what about the President himself?

For a couple of years now I have been toying with ways in which the President might be made more accountable to those whose lives and professional circumstance he crucially affects. While I do not think that his power can be fully shared by any legislative process, I do think that his own tenure should be at risk if he is to enjoy the latitude of executive decision which the job requires.

In thinking through the question of the President's responsibility in the case of a disruptive confrontation, I concluded that the power to act on the spot should not be stultified, but that in spite of all the risks of Monday-morning quarterbacks on the faculty, the President should submit his actions to review and should if necessary make the issue one of confidence. If he were to receive a vote of no-confidence he should offer to resign. This conclusion is implicit in my letter to Dean Miller of April, 1969, in which I tried to spell out our thinking about the protection of dissent and the prevention of disruption.

The principle of executive accountability as the price which must be paid for the exercise of executive discretion has, up to now, been formally limited to the power of the trustees to fire the man they hired as president. This is a terribly limited and inhibited power, since it cannot be exercised without running contrary to the expectation of a lifetime tenure. There is no objective occasion or event which invites the appraisal. Even the most decorous and covert effort to remove an unsatisfactory president is at best a matter of intense personal anguish to everyone concerned.

Since it is likely to be resorted to only after deep rumblings of widespread dissatisfaction have been voiced in several quarters, the chances of concealing the reasons for premature retirement are very slight. If the malaise has erupted into rude, crude, and unattractive challenge, then of course the trustees are likely to get their defensive backs up, just to prove that they cannot be pushed around and that the institution will not be governed by mob rule. So, the worse the disease, the harder the cure.

The essence of the problem is that, while there is legal accountability to the trustees, there is no orderly way in which those most significantly affected by mal-administration can invoke trustee action within a measurable time, without open challenge to the stability of the institution and the integrity of its processes.

It seems to me that the only way this problem can be solved is to require the periodic, explicit renewal of a president's tenure. I happen to think that ten or twelve years or so is about enough anyway, although there is no generalization valid for all times and places and people. More important than the length of average term, however, is the need for some shorter interval which permits periodic reassessment as a matter of course, without waiting for or requiring invidious or disruptive public complaint. Unless there is some such arrangement the hope for genuine accountability at all levels of authority is illusory.

I think Yale would be better off if it were understood that the trustees would make a systematic reappraisal and explicit consideration of the President's reappointment at some specified interval. This might be seven years after the initial appointment, perhaps at a somewhat shorter interval thereafter. I would urge the trustees right now to consider adoption of such a policy. This would mean termination of my present appointment a year from June and an explicit judgment about the wisdom of my reappointment by that time. Under present circumstances the effect would be to make the office more attractive not only for initial appointment but also for continuation in it.

Of course, the trustees could not, and should not, abdicate their ultimate responsibility for the exercise of their best judgment about the best interests of the institution. Occasions have arisen, and may well arise again, where defiance of popular student and faculty opinion is in fact justified by an issue of principle, just as may be the defiance of alumni or public opinion. Reservation of this duty and right, however, does not justify insulation of either the President or the trustees from a periodic, systematic assessment of what student and faculty opinion is.

Such accountability from top to bottom of the institution would require startlingly new measures for full disclosure of the meetings at which decisions were taken and unorthodox revision of the terms of Presidential appointment. Disturbing as they may seem from the perspective of inherited tradition, I would urge with great conviction that they would be far more consistent with the nature of a free academic community, and the administrative leadership it requires, than would the sharing of faculty and administrative responsibility for academic and institutional policies.

If such real accountability were achieved, then I have no doubt whatsoever that consultation would become regular, widespread, and serious. This should include formal as well as informal participation, including elected groups where appropriate. No one with any sense, let alone pride and ambition, could fail to take seriously the importance of adequate consultation with those to whom he would in fact be held accountable at periodic intervals. Sometimes the processes of consultation will be best served by an elective process; sometimes it will best be done by trying deliberately to impanel a group with a greater variety of interests and viewpoints than would probably emerge from majority vote. Also, there are mixed solutions, relying in part on ballot, in part on administrative selection. Most important, there should be no exclusive channel of communication or opinion, nor any requirement that all consultation should be formal.

If it were limited for the most part to consultative arrangements, "legitimacy" might lose some of its rigidity. Even if ultimate responsibility should lie with the full-time faculty and administration, subject only to review by the trustees, consultative participation is both good education for the participants and essential if the institution is to be alert to its own needs in a fast changing society.

I make these somewhat radical proposals because while I do respect and share the dissatisfaction with a governance which seems free to ignore the will of the governed, I think that the sharing of faculty and administrative power with students on a widely dispersed democratic basis would be a disaster for our kind of academic institution. I urge much more strenuous examination of techniques of accountability. They would be more fitting for university governance than would techniques for the sharing of ultimate responsibility with the transient student constituency. In order to further serious consideration of these possibilities, I submit the concrete proposals concerning disclosure and the terms of presidential appointment as worthy of consideration. Much more thought and inquiry is in order before such notions could harden into concrete proposals. They seem to me, however, to point in a direction far more promising than expecting actual direction of university affairs to come from a participatory democracy in which only a minority would participate, a representative democracy which would be unlikely to be truly representative, or the substitution of a legislative power for what are inherently executive responsibilities.

94

THE STUDENT
AND HIS POWER

D. BRUCE JOHNSTONE

STUDENT POWER is a provocative slogan. To the simple and the anxious, it may call to mind nothing but a mob of long-haired youth storming the administration building. To the politically paranoid, student power, like black power, is construed as a rallying cry of conspiratorial forces and their youthful dupes bent on the overthrow of the American way of life. To many faculty and administrators, the students' demand for power is more confusing and frustrating than sinister. Student militancy seems to be the result of a great range of irritations, at times bearing little apparent relation to each other or to the traditional mission of higher education and only rarely accompanied by coherent suggestions for reform. This disenchantment may be directed at alleged curricular irrelevance, at the increasingly outmoded restrictions upon students' private lives, or at the academic establishment in general as symbolic of authority, the status quo, racism, militarism, or any other objects of youthful ire.

Yet, "student power" is more than a simple slogan for the articulation of a social liberalism and a vague disenchantment with higher education. Fundamental to the militancy of any disenchanted group—of whatever color, age, or political inclination—is the helpless frustration of powerlessness. The disenchanted perceive themselves unable not only to influence events but to gain even so much as a respectful recognition from the encroaching environment.

At the heart of student militancy, then, is the question of the proper decision-making role of the student within our institutions of higher education. The analyses and proposals directed at this question and emanating from students, faculty, and administrators alike, however, have viewed student participation in a strikingly narrow perspective. Student power, meaning here the capacity to influence the decision-making processes of the institution, has been viewed almost exclusively in a formal, quasi-legalistic sense.

Reprinted from the Journal of Higher Education, *Vol. XL (March, 1969), pp. 205-18. Copyright © 1969 by the Ohio State University Press and reprinted with its permission.*

The positive exercise of this power—the capacity to influence educational policy—has been restricted to student government and, more recently, to student inclusion on faculty governing committees. The negative exercise of this power has been preoccupied with the students' personal and civil (but only occasionally their academic) rights by seeking to remove from administrative prerogative the traditional practices associated with *in loco parentis.*

It is this author's contention that the very nature of our higher educational institutions virtually precludes any truly meaningful student influence through the formal decision-making machinery of the institution. Where student power is channeled through formal, high level, or all-college decision-making bodies, the result is likely to be either the token representation of a student or two on an existing governing committee or the relegation of student power to those matters such as social activities and student behavior which are least threatening to the academic establishment. Token representation, while politically astute and a potential mechanism for student-faculty communication, is not likely to change the most fundamental problems which underlie student disenchantment. The result, rather, may be to accentuate the polarization of the students and the academic establishment. Channeling student authority into safe areas of high visibility and emotional impact may momentarily appease the demand for student power, but will continue to exclude the student population from the decision-making processes which most affect its educational experience.

If there is a case for student participation in matters of educational policy (and I believe there is, although that case is not the thesis of this paper), then such participation must be sought less through these mechanisms of formal governance and more through informal influence and lower level decision-making processes. By "lower level," I refer to academic policy at the level of the individual course, the department, or the division. Examples of "informal influence" would include the students' market power of choosing or rejecting departments, courses, and teachers; student evaluation of the faculty; and student-run experimental universities which might educate both students and faculty in the realities and the possibilities of alternative subject matter and teaching procedures.

These and other mechanisms for student participation in institutional decision-making, while indirect, informal, and far less visible than the student senate or the joint student-faculty committee, are nevertheless within the range of influence of institutional policy. I believe that the academic establishment can institute means of encouraging and, to a degree, guiding this kind of student power just as it has, in the past, derived course and credit policies, evaluation procedures, and faculty reward systems which have so effectively excluded the student from influence over academic policy.

I do not wish to imply by these observations any reactionary conspiracy of the establishment. The fault, if there be any, lies partly in a lack of true commitment to the cause of student power, but, more fundamentally, in a myopic perspective on the nature of institutional influence and decision-making. This myopia, in turn, is in large part due to a lack of theoretical models which might describe the actual and potential roles for the student in the total decision-making and influence structure of the college or university. I offer the following elaboration on the above views as a very small contribution to this need.

Probably the most common and most primitive model for furthering student participation—if not student power—is through a communications, or student forum, model. Students are brought before or included upon various permanent or ad hoc committees, both policy-making and investigating. Students are encouraged to debate issues and to formulate resolutions within their own governing bodies and to bring these before the actual policy makers within the academic establishment. Occasionally, students, faculty, and administrators are brought together on an informal level in small groups or within classes. The idea is to "get together," to "hear things out," and to "bridge the communications gap."

There are three major weaknesses in this model of student "power." First, the communications model is predicated upon a peculiarly American refusal to accept the existence of a permanent, fundamental disagreement among reasonable men. We are so accustomed to a monolithic American ideology that we tend to view all lasting conflict as a result either of obstinance or misunderstanding. Be the conflict between the United States and the Soviet Union, between labor and management, or between the academic establishment and the student body, the conflict is viewed as essentially soluble if only the parties could get together, open their minds, and act with reason. What we—the students, the administration, and the public in general—often fail to recognize is that the conflict may, in fact, be quite fundamental. The parties may be communicating very nicely their essential differences, and no additional "getting together" is, in itself, going to have the least effect toward a solution.

A second weakness of the communications model is that it may fail to convey to any but a handful of student leaders and political activists a true sense of participation and influence. The students with ready access to the ears of the establishment may be a most unrepresentative minority—perhaps the "straight" college politicians or perhaps, more recently, the militants, but rarely, for obvious reasons, the great, gray, acquiescent middle. It could be argued, of course, that this middle has little to say and even less concern with being heard. Yet this acquiescence is, itself, a student ethic which may largely be a consequence of the traditional powerlessness of the American college student. It is just as reasonable to argue that if the average student has neither a sense of power nor a concern for his powerlessness, it becomes the responsibility of our institutions to give him alternative forms of power and to make him care for its effective use.

The third and the most fundamental weakness of the communication model is its ambivalence on matters of rights and authority. This problem is revealed by the simple question: What if the establishment should cease to listen? A statement by Samuel B. Gould, chancellor of the State University of New York, is a typical, sympathetic response to the issue of student participation in college governance, yet one which illustrates the dependence of the communications model upon the noblesse of the faculty and administration. He writes:

> Maturity of the student can be nurtured as we draw him into the orbit of decision-making on the campus. . . . Such decisions have to do with academic programs, with adaptations or expansions of calendars, with regulations relating to student life, with experimentation and innovative change.
>
> Granted that the student lacks experiences with most or all of these matters, he is the one who contributes to making them succeed or fall. And so, although he is in no position to make the deciding judgments as to what should be done he can participate in the process that brings about such judgments.[1]

Alternative models, then, must be devised to partially circumvent the potential hypocrisy of this "responsibility on a string." One such model of student participation in academic decision-making vests the students, through some duly elected representative body with a quasi-legal veto power or even complete jurisdiction over certain matters—subject, of course, to the ultimate discretion of a governing body or a state legislature.

The very nature of higher education, however, precludes nearly all matters of academic policy from such authority. This exclusion, far from a simple, conspiratorial maintenance of the status quo, has reasonable bases both in our traditional conception of the educational process and in the very nature of formal institutions. The first basis is both ontological and epistemological: education, we may agree, exists to direct the student toward some cognitive, attitudinal, or vocational goal. Assuming that the student has not yet attained any one of these goals, how can he be in a position to know the knowledge that is of most worth or the means by which this knowledge is to be gained? Would not the student, left entirely to his own devices, tend simply to reinforce his existing interests, inclinations, and prejudices? Thus, while the student's needs and interests are relevant to the goals of education and essential to the process of learning, the ultimate authority over what and how he is to learn must reside with those who are older and wiser.

The second argument for excluding academic policy from those matters over which students may have quasi-legal authority rests on the dependence of formal education upon institutions. All institutions involving physical and human resources formally organized toward a set of goals can

---

[1]Samuel B. Gould, "The Role of the Student in the Life of the University," NASPA, Vol. (October, 1966), p. 54. Second set of italics mine.

exist only with some degree of stability and some semblance of perpetuity. Although change can be built into both the goals and the decision-making procedures, all institutions will seek to maintain these goals and procedures once established. The power to alter severely either the goals or the procedures cannot be placed in the hands of those who would be immune from the consequences of that exercise of power. A student generation of four years, it is said, is too short to be controlled by this anticipation of consequences and might, thus, act in such a manner as to jeopardize the education of future students.

One solution to this dilemma has been to grant students virtual sovereignty within narrowly prescribed domains which pose no threat either to the institution as a corporate person or to the members (as opposed to the clients) of that institution. (Such matters, it might be added, are also matters of responsibility from which both faculty and administration are generally delighted to be free.) Thus, students through their own councils may have complete authority for the establishment and enforcement of most behavioral rules, for running student publications, for chartering student organizations, for inviting speakers to the campus, and for planning social functions.

Student control over these matters is philosophically, educationally, and administratively sound. Yet, with student power confined to these formal, quasi-legal procedures, the effect is to exclude from meaningful student participation the most basic sources of dissatisfaction: the content of the curriculum and the quality of the teaching. It is true that *in loco parentis*, restrictions on political activities, and alleged university collaboration with racism or militarism are all more visible and more vulnerable as targets of student dissent. But, again, we may have a circularity: student powerlessness in academic matters is so thoroughly established throughout our educational system that students may have lost all perspective concerning their potential power and contribution. The fact that students may be unable to articulate what they feel would constitute good teaching or a relevant curriculum in no way invalidates their visceral conviction that teaching is often ineffectual and silly and that curricular content answers more to the needs of graduate schools and departmentalized disciplines than to the needs of a society approaching the twenty-first century. Omission of academic policy from effective student participation, then, is not simply a loss to the students; it is a loss to all of higher education—to those who serve it and to those who support it.

Occasionally an institution reflects a sincere belief that it needs the student in the formulation of academic policy. More prevalent rationales for student participation, however, perpetuate those models in which students play at democracy, form committees, and give free, but often futile, expression to the violations of their personal rights. One such rationale is the thought that formal student government has a direct educational return

99

in the practice of active democracy and in the assumption of greater responsibility. The confinement of that responsibility, however, to the least threatening matters of institutional concern may not only fail to involve the total student body, but may engender a tragic cynicism toward student government and even the democratic process.

A second common rationale for student government is its alleged effect upon student morale. A 1958 study by Alden J. Carr of student participation in teachers' colleges provides a striking example of this rationale. Administrators were asked what they felt to be the "principle favorable effects upon the college" of student participation in policy determination. "Better morale" was by far the most frequent response, cited by 61.4 per cent of administrators, followed by "better cooperation" and "better learning," each named by 28.4 per cent of respondents. By contrast, only 9.3 per cent responded within the category of "contribution of valuable ideas by students."[2] Such findings can only suggest the involvement of students in institutional decision-making as a palliative—a concession to buy off irresponsible students, or a means to channel excessive and potentially disruptive energy into possibly constructive, but at least harmless, student activities.

The current literature is full of statements in favor of student participation in academic matters for the positive rationale that the students have something unique and essential to offer higher education. For the mechanics of this participation, however, we must turn to models other than traditional, formal student government. An increasingly popular model which purports to give students full decision-making citizenship while avoiding the fear of student sovereignty over threatening matters is the inclusion of students as voting members on permanent governing committees. E. G. Williamson and John L. Cowan found 61 per cent of their responding sample placing students on key policy-making committees, 85 per cent of which gave students full voting rights.[3]

Again, however, the question of real power arises: does a minority of two or three students against ten or twelve faculty members constitute meaningful student power or mere tokenism? My very question, of course, implies a "them against us" polarization between students and faculty or administration. But is such polarization inevitable? And, if so, isn't the joint governing committee still as good a place as any to confront issues and to seek solutions of mutual accord? Indeed, we can conceive of a model of governance where students are included not as students, but, rather, as full members of an academic community. This utopian model, of which

---

[2]Alden J. Carr, *Student Participation in College Policy Determination and Administration* (Washington, D.C.: American Association of Colleges for Teacher Education, 1959), p. 53.

[3]E.G. Williamson and John L. Cowan, *The American Student's Freedom of Expression: A Research Appraisal* (Minneapolis: University of Minnesota Press, 1966), p. 134.

Antioch College is the best-known living approximation, may well remain the ideal form of college governance. But such a model must assume no intrinsic, extraordinary differences of interest which would divide those permanent, producing members of the community and the temporary, client members of the community.

However, as cited above, there are just such differences between those who are to be changed and those who are to change them—between those for whom a given institution is a way of life and a livelihood and those for whom the institution has been freely chosen to dispense a desired service.

In claiming real and legitimate differences between students and the academic establishment, I am not advocating a stultifying polarization. I strongly support measures designed to break down artificial barriers and to insure an equality of respect for all members of the academic community. But this is not the same as urging an equality of decision-making roles. Nor would the student necessarily gain by an erasure of the distinctions between him and the faculty with respect to authority and responsibility. Theodore P. Green of Amherst College claims, in fact, that both the student and the institution gain most by maintaining the "independent adversary" role for the student. Only in such a role can the student maintain both his power and his unique perspective upon the problems of higher education.[4]

Although an essential polarization of interest between students and the faculty or administration may eliminate Antioch as a general model for student participation, polarization does not, in itself, invalidate the joint committee model of student power. What does invalidate this model as a mechanism for student power is the very nature of the collegial organization. Colleges and universities, at least to some very significant degree, operate on a collegial process of decision-making, depending upon member consensus rather than upon the hierarchial authority structure of the classical bureaucracy. No collegial body can tolerate prolonged, open conflict or a permanent polarization of interest. For students to be included upon a collegial governing council, they must either be rigidly controlled by distinct minority status or their participation must, again, be confined to councils dealing in matters which can pose no threat to the interests of the academic establishment.

For student power to be real to the student body, effective as a force for the continual improvement and updating of the academic program, and, at the same time, compatible with our present institutionalized forms of higher education, we need to expand greatly our conceptions of power and influence. In particular, we must consider the myriad of influence channels which operate indirectly, informally, or out of the public eye. The following examples are models only of the crudest sort, but they are, I hope, sugges-

---

[4]Theodore P. Greene, "John Cotton, Anne Hutchinson, and the 'Student Power' Movement," in *Stress and Campus Response: Current Issues in Higher Education, 1968,* G. Kerry Smith (ed.) (San Francisco: Jossey-Bass Inc., 1968), pp. 99-105.

tive of the potential which lies in this expanded perception of student power and influence.

Power through lower level communications—Where communication between students and faculty is most needed is not at the all-college level, but at the level of the division, the department, and the individual course. Joint planning of individual courses may be quite difficult to institutionalize, as such, but it is rather extraordinary that more procedures have not been devised to bring students into departmental and devisional policy-making. Charles B. Neff urges that the department be the primary focus for the expansion of student participation in policy-making.[5] Not only is this the level where the action is, but it is also the level at which students can make their most concrete and valuable contributions. Furthermore lower level decision-making, while no less collegial, should be less visible and less constrained by legality and precedent than formal, college level governing councils and therefore less vulnerable to conflict. Finally, lower level participation would allow more students to participate actively in policy-making and would be more attractive to those students who, on principle, eschew formal student government or campus politics.

Power through individualized programs—Much of the legitimate resistance to student power in academic policy is directed at the notion of a student body or its governing councils as a collective decision maker which could then impose its conception of educational relevance or academic procedures upon other students, both present and future. There is, however, far less resistance to individualized programming, independent study, credit by examination, and other devices designed to break the academic lockstep. The students' lack of power is, in large part, a result of their subordination to rigid degree requirements and spurious practices of evaluation. The freeing of learning from these constraints constitutes not only a significant curricular innovation but also a considerable transfer of power from the faculty to the students.

Power through consumer preference—The significance of the students' market power effected through their choice to elect or not to elect a certain college, department, course, or professor is greatly debated in the literature of higher education. Clark Kerr attributes considerable power to the student-as-consumer. He writes:

> The system of electives gives them [the students] a chance to help determine in which areas and disciplines a university will grow. Their choices, as consumers, guide university expansion and contraction, and this process is far superior to a more rigid guild system of producer determination as in medicine where quotas are traditional. Also students, by their patronage, designate the university teachers. . . . In a large university a quarter of the faculty

---

[5]Charles B. Neff, "The Administrative Challenge of the New Student Activism," *Journal of Higher Education*, Vol. 39 (February, 1968), pp. 69-76.

may be selected by the students to do half or more of the actual teaching; the students also "select" ten percent or more to do almost none at all.[6]

Other observers have minimized the market power of the student.[7] I tend to feel that the effective market power of the student has been minimal except in institutions heavily dependent upon a local clientele or upon professional and inservice training. I also believe, however, that the market power model holds great promise for effective student influence over the nature and diversity of higher education. Policies which could greatly enhance this power include individualizing the academic program, encouraging credit by examination, facilitating a better matching of students with institutions and with academic majors, allowing credit for work done in certain extra-institutional activities, encouraging and subsidizing a student evaluation of courses and instructors, providing massive student loans and equalizing the cost burden between public and private institutions, and instituting a faculty reward system which is somewhat more responsive to the students. The last-named device deserves elaboration below.

Power through the faculty reward system—Few proposals will elicit as much negative reaction as those which suggest a role for the student in matters of hiring and firing, promotions, and faculty salaries. Yet, there seems to be no good reason why a properly designed student evaluation of courses and instructors should not have some place in these matters. The more serious problem in tampering with the reward system is that we know so little of how it works. Every faculty member responds differently to a complex set of rewards including salary, outside research grants, teaching assignments, reputation within his profession, reputation among his departmental colleagues, recognition and praise from the administration, and feedback from his students.

Unfortunately, student feedback—even when reinforced by published course evaluations—seems to be diminishing in importance as a source of reward. Yet some of the proposals cited above, particularly those referring to the students' market power, may indirectly enhance the students' role in the reward system. For example, a program where student and instructor devise a course of study in preparation for an externally administered examination might restore some balance of power between the two roles. The instructor loses his power of the grade; furthermore, he is now subject to some punishment by the student should the student fail the examina-

[6]Clark Kerr, *The Uses of the University* (Cambridge, Massachusetts: Harvard University Press, 1963), pp. 21-22. A similar, more expanded view is taken by John D. Millett in *The Academic Community: An Essay on Organization* (New York: McGraw-Hill Book Company, Inc., 1962), pp. 106-48.

[7]For examples, see Joh W. Dykstra, "Consumer Protection in the Higher Education Marketplace," *Phi Delta Kappan,* Vol. 47 (April, 1966), pp. 446-48; John J. Corson, *The Governance of Colleges and Universities* (New York: McGraw-Hill Book Company, 1960), p. 142; and David Riesman, *Constraint and Variety in American Education* (New York: Doubleday and Company, Inc., 1958), pp. 1-16.

tion under his tutelage. Such a program has been in operation at Lake Forest, Allegheny, and Colorado colleges and is an excellent example of the potential impact of curricular and procedural innovation upon the influence structure of a college.[8]

Power through the experimental college—Perhaps we are wasting time by instituting procedures for giving students a say in academic matters when they have such difficulty (although no more than most faculty) expressing what it is they mean by "relevant" and "meaningful" educational experiences. Why not first let them work out some alternatives to their current experiences and discover what they want, what resource demands are involved, and what administrative procedures are necessary? James Andrews describes the Student Experimental College at San Francisco State as a potential mechanism for profound impact on the parent institution. It not only allows a full expression of what students are responding to; it also is educating the students into some of the bureaucratic and financial realities which seem to settle on the freest of universities.[9]

Power through expression of dissent—Campus protests in a great variety of forms, "underground" publications, and ad hoc student committees for the changing of this and that must also be considered important mechanisms for student influence. With the possible exception of practices which lead to violence or the restriction of rights of others, all of these devices have vital counterparts in the influence structure of the general polity. When we consider the legitimate importance of lobbying, pressure groups, demonstrations, and so forth at all levels of government, it is strange that these same activities are often considered illegitimate or aberrant when engaged in by students for the purpose of changing the educational system.

To make these activities an integral part of institutional decision-making would, of course, destroy their very usefulness—and possibly the institution as well. But the institution can anticipate and even encourage many such activities, preparing itself to react not out of fear or anger, but out of a healthy respect for a very real power which should and must be listened to.

There is nothing substantially new in these six models of informal, indirect, and lower level student power. What is new is to consider these essentially academic and curricular policies as potential mechanisms for bringing the total student body into an effective decision-making role with respect to the very nature of their educational experience. It is my belief that such mechanisms constitute a far more fruitful approach to the entire set of issues concerning student power than do the traditional models of formal student government and joint governing committees.

---

[8]William G. Cole, "Breaking the Grade-and-Credit Mold," in *The Challenge of Curricular Change* (New York: College Entrance Examination Board, 1966), pp. 42-50.

[9]James Andrews, "The Student Experimental College: Its Impact on Campus Culture," *NASPA*, Vol. 5 (October, 1967), pp. 119-23. The issues of power and dissent are so complex and interrelated that one can only conjecture at this time whether the 1968-69 disruptions at San Francisco State corroborate, rebut, or fail to test Andrew's assertion.

STUDENTS IN THE
POLICY PROCESS

JAY C. SHAFFER

AS UNREST in our institutions of higher learning reaches new heights, some observations need to be made about students as participants in the university policy process. Let it be understood from the outset that these observations are not empirically documented. In fact, the purpose of this article is to urge that, among other things, research be done in the field of student participation.

The first proposition is that there is a significant proportion of college students who are dissatisfied with the state of society in general and with the condition of the university in particular. The second is that there exists a relatively small sample of students who can be described as "activists," and who are willing to devote a great deal of time and effort to the promotion of change in the university. Further, these activists have every intention of pursuing such activity whether or not university administrators and faculty recognize them as legitimate participants. The third proposition is that more and more university administrators and faculty are beginning to recognize students as legitimate participants.[1] To be sure, this admission is often hedged with qualifications, but, nonetheless, students are being placed on top-level policy committees, allowed to peruse the budget, given much greater authority over parietal rules, consulted in the selection of new presidents, and, in some institutions, formally seated with the board of trustees.

This formal integration of students into the university policy process, a dramatic development, results from the conjunction of a complex array of factors: student pressure and protests; realization by administrators that in an era of rapid change, age and wisdom are not necessarily correlated;

---

[1] For the balance of this article, the term "administration" will be used instead of the more cumbersome "university administration and faculty." The arguments are directed both to administrators and to faculty members who deal with students in a policy-making context.

Reprinted from the Journal of Higher Education, *XLI (May, 1970), pp. 341-49. Copyright © 1970 by the Ohio State University Press and reprinted with its permission.*

genuine belief that administrative decisions will be better decisions if the comments and concerns of the people they affect are sought out in advance; and, perhaps most important, recognition that students are going to participate in one way or another, and that it is better to have several students sitting on committees than several hundred of them sitting in the administration building.

While there is exhaustive literature on both student activism and the capacity of students to deal with academic issues, little exploration has been made of the implications of actually admitting students to the policy process. Such an exploration is the purpose of this article. No attempt will be made to establish a justification for student participation. It is a given; the implications are the topic.

The *first* implication of student "legitimization" is that there is an immediate need for the actual organization of student participation. After all, on most campuses it is not possible to let any and all interested parties participate at will. Not only must the number of participating students be brought down to manageable proportions, but those who do participate must be representative; that is, each one should be acting for a substantial group of like-minded peers.

The immediate impulse is to turn to the regular student government. Its members are elected by the student body, and it is really the only formally existing vehicle for organizing participation. Unfortunately, student government usually bears the bitter fruits of past university policy. Years of suppression and paternalism have left it emasculated. It is probably peopled with vapid collegiate types and concerned with trivia; its elections marked by sparse turn-out and even less democracy; its activities held in contempt by activists and generally ignored by almost everyone else. Somehow it must be made attractive to the students who are intent on promoting change; otherwise, they will attempt to influence policy through a disorganized system of multiple access points. The result would be satisfactory neither to the students nor to the university.

But how is a student government made attractive? A university administration that wishes to suppress a student government is not faced with a serious problem. Turning it into a vital, responsive vehicle for policy participation is another matter. The solution to the problem demands recognition of an elementary fact: students are just like other people. They tend to concern themselves with things that affect their interests. They pay attention to a "government" only to the extent that they see that government effectively influencing issues of personal importance. David Fellman treats this point well as he comments on professors who participate so lackadaisically in university-wide faculty meetings:

> Like the nonvoter in the body politic, the nonparticipating professor is almost wholly impervious to moralistic preachments about where his duties lie. Just as "get-out-and-vote" campaigns have very little to do with actual turnout

at the polls, so do professors respond negatively to mere appeals to their sense of obligation. Like most other people, professors respond to the push and pull of their interests, not to mere exhortation.[2]

Exactly! A vital student government is not developed by urging the student public to be better campus citizens, or by asking student leaders to be more representative and responsible. Students at large will vote in elections and enforce responsiveness only when self-interest demands it. The student leadership is somewhat different—from time to time a sense of obligation may lead it to attempt projects of significance and to achieve rapport with the electorate. But these things will be assured only when they are prerequisites for the political survival of the leadership. In any case, to argue that power should not be invested in the student government until it has first been browbeaten into a state of "responsible representativeness" places the cart before the horse. The absence of power and influence is itself the principal reason why student government is not representative in the first place. It is a causal relationship stemming from ordinary human nature.

If students, then, are to see the student government as an effective means of participation, it is necessary, first of all, to invest extensive power in the hands of the government permanently. Second, when this power is exercised, the decisions must be honored. This point is crucial. The student electorate has been accustomed no doubt to seeing the decisions and suggestions of its government unilaterally reversed or ignored by the university administration on the grounds that the action "does not have campus support." This must stop. If students feel that some administrator will step in when the government acts irresponsibly, then the government will never become responsive to its own electorate. The actions of the government should be accepted instantly and without question as the voice of the student body. If this is done vigorously several times in cases where student opinion is heavily opposed to the government's action, the government will soon become remarkably representative as its members come under fire from constituents. This process of reorientation will mean a difficult time for all concerned, but that price must be paid.

The student government can be made even more attractive to the activists by granting it a substantial amount of money. This money should be allocated annually from student fees, and should be in an amount equal, at a minimum, to either $5,000 or $2.00 for every full-time student, whichever is higher. (For example, a student government representing twenty-five thousand students should be allotted at least $50,000.) This is guaranteed to arouse continuing student interest. It will also have certain effects upon the nature of student government activity, which will be discussed later.

[2]David Fellman, "The Academic Community," in *Whose Goals for American Higher Education?* Charles G. Dobbins and Calvin B. T. Lee (eds.), (Washington, D.C.: American Council on Education, 1968), pp. 115-16.

Finally, the university administration should give public evidence of its regard for the student government. The principal officers of the student government should be treated in the same way that a dean is treated, and should be provided with office space that is as liberally appointed as a dean's. This must be done whether or not the student officers are "good" officers, just as a dean is entitled to certain prerogatives simply because he is a dean, and independent of whether he is a "good" dean. In other words, the administration must act as if it means what it says about students being true participants. A policy of telling students that they are effective participants, without according them the prestige accorded to other established participants, is doomed.

All of this will have a salutary effect on the responsiveness of the government, on turn-out at the polls, and on the quality and the nature of the students seeking leadership in the government. The new sources of influence vested in the student government will tend to attract high quality leadership material from the ranks of the moderate activists. However, no one should be so foolish as to suppose that a student government, even a very powerful one, would attract all those in the activist camp. There is a good reason for this. On most campuses, activists come in three varieties. The first group can be called "system" activists. They accept the proposition that change can be effected within the system and are reluctant to promote their ends by public mass actions like demonstrations and sit-ins. They are usually opposed to illegal action. The second group can be described as "radical" activists. They reject the idea that change can be produced by operating within the system. They believe that mass action is necessary and are often willing to undertake illegal action. It is important to realize that these two activist groups are interested in the same changes. That is, if their means differ, their ends do not. Further, the ends in which they are interested are tacitly supported by a large segment of the rest of the student population who are not activists at all. It is a great mistake to equate student apathy with student conservatism.

The third type of activists can be called anarchists. Their means are similar to those of the radical activists, but their ends are different. They are not so much interested in reforming the university as they are in destroying it and the larger society is supposedly represents. Fortunately, the anarchistic activists have significant strength on relatively few campuses.

This trichotomy can also be treated as a continuum. Suppression of student activism in all its forms would probably lead system activists to become radical activists and radical activists to become anarchists.

The aim of student government revitalization should be to bring the system activists into control of the organized means of student participation. The radical activists, of course, will resist any effort to integrate them into the system. However, if the system activists operate shrewdly, they can maintain the respect of the radical activists. The radical activists then become a sort of loyal opposition that keeps the moderates honest, and prevents them from "selling out" to the university administration. Of course, the moderates will always find the radicals useful as a club to hold over the head of the administration. Further, the more successful the moderates are at producing change, the more effective they will be at moderating the more violent tactics of the radicals. Thus, the trichotomy begins to operate as a reverse continuum. The more effective the system activists are, the more they are joined by former radical activists, and the anarchists find themselves increasingly isolated.

The *second* implication of student legitimization is that the university must provide for *effective* student participation. Students do not want simply to participate in the policy process, they want to participate effectively. They want to see decisions influenced by their own ideas, comments, and actions. The fact is, however, that students are inherently ineffective participants. If they are left to operate alone without special advantages and assistance, they will not affect policy outcomes. The resulting frustration can be disastrous—worse than if students had been flatly denied the opportunity to participate in the first place. When rising expectations are smashed, the response is especially bitter.

There are several excellent reasons why students are handicapped in dealing with other policy groups. To begin with, students are unsophisticated about the policy process itself. They have incomplete and inaccurate conceptions of who has power to do what, what groups influence which kinds of policy, and how the university is financed, organized, and operated. They have little experience as policy makers or diplomats, and do not have the essential skills of a veteran participant. Their very idea of how reform occurs is often highly simplistic, and based upon the belief that the only prerequisite for change is proof that the current policy is immoral.

Second, students are transients. This creates serious problems of continuity. Students who achieve an understanding of the process soon graduate, and their successors do not benefit from the experience. Thus, the long-term participants in the process have a standing advantage over them.

Third, students do not have access to the information essential for effective participation. If they do get it, they do not have the means to interpret it or use it to develop independent proposals.

Fourth, student government usually does not have the facilities and staff normally available to other process participants. A government cannot buy much in the way of electric typewriters, or duplicating machines, or desk calculators, or computer time, or telephone service on an annual budget of a few thousand dollars. Nor can it assemble a staff of research personnel and professional advisers.

Fifth, students are usually students first and policy participants second. They have heavy academic responsibilities that limit their efforts as policy makers, especially around examination periods. Further, they are usually away from campus during breaks and over the summer, while the process grinds on without them.

Finally, students are sometimes treated in a condescending manner by the people with whom they are participating. A university policy of student legitimization is not simultaneously accepted by all parties concerned, and the nonstudent members of a university committee can simply refuse to communicate with the student members.

The university must attempt to remedy these disabilities and it must do so as an integral part of accepting student participation itself. Student naiveté should be met by offering a regular academic course dealing with the university policy process. The treatment should be thorough, analytical, and accurate, from the state legislature right down to the local SDS. It should sharpen student perception and show the need for adopting a professional style, but without attempting to induce students into establishment viewpoints. It should be designed to attract activists of every variety.

To close the "fact gap," the university must disclose its background information and possible policy alternatives. The administrator responsible for student relations should constantly insist on the right of the appropriate student participators to be adequately informed well in advance of impending policy decisions.

The suggestion that student government be granted money has been noted earlier. This money can be used by the government to purchase adequate equipment and secretarial service, and to undertake a host of programs that will increase its prestige and efficacy in the eyes of students. Further, the money will enable the government to commission investigations into various issue areas, to hire persons of special expertise (e.g., a lobbyist to deal with the state legislature), and to employ permanent staff professionals who can ferret out the complex details of university operation and other information that will inevitably be withheld from students. This professional staff will also help offset the disadvantages of student transiency.

The student time problem is particularly difficult. The university should consider granting academic credit for policy participation. This would allow the student leadership to take less than a full course load, and would consequently provide them with some additional time.

Finally, condescension should be fought by public promotion of confidence in student capabilities, by encouraging nonstudent participants to cooperate, and, if necessary, by removing the uncooperative from policy areas of student interest.

The *third,* and last, implication is that a wise university administration will seek better information about this new group it has integrated into the policy process. There are countless surveys, books, and articles on trustees, presidents, deans, faculty members, and all the other traditional groups that operate to influence university policy. The number of current, full-length books or studies on student participation is virtually nil. The university should know more about its students than just their age, sex, and home address. It should have some knowledge of their feelings, attitudes, and inclinations. It especially should know more about the student leadership—how it emerges, changes, operates, and thinks. This article alone unabashedly rests upon a host of inductive assumptions. Nearly all of them need to be empirically tested. The student political arena is no longer so trivial as to be dealt with on the basis of simple conjecture.

Such are the implications of involving students in the policy process. They are not trifling implications, but they do seem to be often overlooked as universities rush to accommodate their rebellious charges. The task is more formidable than it appears, and in that respect this new era in the evolution of the academic community is no different from most of its predecessors.

THE STRUCTURE
OF UNIVERSITIES

CHARLES FRANKEL

THE CLAIM that students should participate in the major decision-making processes of colleges or universities is a political one. Its justification, if it has any, is the same as that which lies behind the demand of subordinate groups who constitute a majority in other domains of society to have a say about the conditions of their life and work. The justification, in short, is the general one that democratic principles call for the establishment of student power in higher education.

But is this what "democratic principles" do entail? Indeed, do they apply to institutions of learning? Are colleges and universities sufficiently like cities or national governments, or unions or factories, to justify the use of the same political arguments in relation to them? Or are they so different that a different set of principles applies to them, in part or in whole?

Weaving through most demands for "student power," or, for that matter, some demands for "faculty power," there are recurrent assumptions. They are worth listing.

1) A university consists of separate groups or blocs. Administrators and trustees form one bloc, the faculty a second, the students a third. The relationships between these blocs are essentially like the relationships between other groups in a political situation. Power is the name of the game, and each fights to get a larger share of it. If justice is to be served, therefore, the subordinate groups have to fight for more power. In a university, this means that faculty and students form a natural alliance. They are, in effect, the workers and peasants of the university, facing its entrenched ruling class, the trustees, together with their paid lackeys, the administrators.

2) Universities are not democratic organizations, but they should be. It is a sign of the hypocrisy of present-day society that it talks about individual rights and majority rule but denies the members of the largest group in the universities—the students—any voice in their government.

3) Accordingly, government by a board of trustees, supported by an ad-

Reprinted, with permission, from Charles Frankel, Education and the Barricades *(New York: W. W. Norton & Co., 1968), pp. 40-59.*

ministration, must be abolished or radically altered. Students and professors should make the major decisions, and the administration should be reduced to doing the housework. At the very least, trustees and administrators should be forced to share their power. For it is not clear what trustees do, or why they have any rights over a university.

All of these assumptions have an initial plausibility about them. Yet the first, it seems to me, is a portrait of a university painted with an axe. The second is a tangle of laudable ideals and loose political philosophy. As for the third, it makes some interesting practical recommendations that are worth discussing. But if we are going to pursue them, it is important to do so for the right reasons, and most of the reasons that are given are wrong.

There are, of course, some characteristics of "class conflict" within universities. Professors bargain for their salaries with administrators. The general level of faculty salaries is influenced by pressures from the faculty. Conditions of work, such as the number of courses taught, are subjects of negotiation. The faculty as a group maintains a watchful eye over the administration to be sure that it does not trample on the faculty's rights. Professors think that administrators don't know what's going on. Administrators think that professors don't understand them. All of this resembles an employer-employee relationship.

Yet the resemblance is limited, and if it is taken as the clue to the essential nature of the relationship between faculty and administration, it is violently misleading. The professor has tenure: after he has passed certain signposts, he cannot be fired from his job short of misconduct, and not always then. His equity in his job is as firm as if he had bought it. And the president of his university can give him fewer orders about what to do with his job than his town council can give him about what to do with his house and land.

There is a fundamental respect in which the administrators of a university are in a different position from the managers of a company. The university administrators cannot create a total plan of work, define jobs within it, and then assign individual workers to them. Of course, now that labor unions have the power they have, managers cannot do this as easily as they once could. But the difference between their position and that of university administrators is nevertheless very great. The product of a factory is a corporate product to which individuals contribute. The product of a university is many separate, individual products, for which the corporate arrangements provide protection and support, but for which the individuals have basic responsibility.

The university administrator, by and large, has to deal with people who are intent on their own work, who have bargaining power in their own individual right, who have entrenched positions and feudal retainers around them, and who carry with them bundles of traditional freedoms and antique privileges on which they can call in time of trouble. Usually, it's no contest:

113

the administrator is out of his league. By cajolery, by the allocation of funds, every once in a while by the power of his ideas, he can try to bring some system and purpose into the division of faculty labor. But he doesn't run the plant. This is a reason, perhaps it is the most important reason, why students so often fail to get a fair shake educationally. Universities are intensely individualistic in their structure and spirit. It is not impossible but it is difficult to bring the individualists that compose them together to study and agree on their collective business.

In brief, a university, though a hierarchy, is a discontinuous hierarchy. The faculty is one hierarchy, the administration another, and the two hierarchies do different things, generally speaking. Where their activities overlap or conflict, there has to be a settlement. But on the whole, universities manage to keep going because each group recognizes its place. The relation between administration and faculty is not a relation between superiors and subordinates, and certainly not a relation between employer and employees. It is a constitutional arrangement for the separation of powers.

The model of employer-employee relations, with its overtones of "class conflict," probably applies best, indeed, not to the relations between administration and faculty, but to the relations between senior professors and junior members of the teaching staff. Here some of the traditional—indeed, the nineteenth-century—powers of the boss over the worker apply. The junior teacher's assignment is given to him, and he depends on his boss for his bread and career. Because there has been a shortage of labor in the academic market-place in recent years, junior teachers have a somewhat better bargaining position than they once did. Nevertheless, the young instructor or professor without tenure is the closest thing we have, in a contemporary American university, to the old-fashioned exploited worker.

Where, then, do students fit into this situation? The fact is that there is no analogy from any other human collectivity that quite applies to their position in a university. Consumer, worker, recipient of favors, protected son— the student is all of these, and none. He is a consumer, yes, but an unlucky one: he has to pass tests laid down by the seller before he is allowed to leave with the prize he came to purchase. Is he a worker? There are similarities. He has to submit to the rules and regulations of the management, and produce what it wants him to produce. But he does not turn over what he produces and get a wage in return. What he produces—certain skills and attitudes, a demonstrated mastery of a field of knowledge, a set of qualities of mind he did not have when he entered—these are his, not the management's, and they are presumably for his principal benefit, not the management's.

Is he, then, in the position of a beneficiary, a recipient of favors, an object of philanthropy? The student cannot entirely dodge this analogy. Even when he pays for his education, he doesn't pay its full cost, and he certainly receives a great many services intended to keep him healthy and happy. And yet, as a citizen in an affluent democracy, as a twentieth-century man with a full quota of human rights, the student is only receiving what the society, it is now generally held, is under a fair obligation to give him. Besides, it needs him for its own purposes, and it needs him trained.

So perhaps a better analogy is that the student is like the protected son in the family, loved and guarded while he is prepared for his future role. In English-speaking countries particularly, the university has in fact been expected to serve some of the functions of a surrogate family, and the student has been expected to submit to some of the restraints of living in the parental nest. But one need only state this analogy to see that it illuminates only a part of the story. All along people have known that, as Mr. Dooley said, at the age when a boy is fit to go to college, he isn't fit to be kept at home. The college has represented the parents, but it has also served the social function of easing the student out of the family and into the public world.

Probably the best analogy is simply that of the apprentice in the old medieval guild. It applies in certain ways to graduate students. The difficulty, however, is that it does not really apply to undergraduates. Essentially, undergraduate students are going through the first initiation rites of the scholarly guild. But they are going through them with a difference. Very few of them go on to full membership in the guild, and no one administers these rites to them with the expectation that most of them are in training to be full-time scholars. What has happened, apparently, is that the scholarly guild has managed to convince the other guilds that its initiation rites are generally useful to everybody else, and not least to the initiate himself. This may be right or it may be wrong, but it means that the college student is not an apprentice in the traditional sense.[1] We are forced to the conclusion that students are—students! It is a status all to itself, and no other word describes it as well.

This may seem, undoubtedly it does seem, an exceedingly long way around to a tautology. But taking this long way around is illuminating. For most of the odd, novel, or shocking things that are being said about the condition of students in the United States today, and many of the discussions taking place about the re-allocation of powers within universities, depend on the application of loose and unexamined analogies, drawn from other types of social organization, to the structure of institutions of learning.

Thus, to take a doctrine that has achieved growing currency, students are not an "exploited" group. It is possible to say other things about them: for example, that they are in the grip of a punishing and misconceived examination and admissions system that puts too many of the wrong kinds of

---

[1] This may seem to apply only to students in liberal arts colleges, and not to those in vocationally oriented schools like those of agriculture, nursing, or home economics. But even in these schools, the emphasis is on the mastery of general skills and broad fields of learning, and not on picking up the tricks of a trade.

pressure on them; that they are neglected; that, in many places, they are perversely miseducated; that they are harassed, constrained, and subject to indignities ranging from Victorian rules in dormitories to forced service in the army. Some or all of these are defensible statements. But they do not mean that students are "exploited," if the word means that anyone is profiting from them at their expense. As those who have experienced exploitation know, it usually involves a condition more painful to endure than boring or "irrelevant" classes. When this doctrine is propounded by students in revolt, or by middle-aged people who claim to speak for them, it can encourage, among those who remember the Depression, a feeling that there really is a "generation-gap." And to students who are today trying to rise out of poverty, and to struggle against exploitation, it can give the impression that members of the more fortunate middle class are indeed insulated from reality.

Nor is the larger version of the doctrine of the exploited student any more persuasive. The word "exploitation" has been stretched so that it is used to describe the process by which young men and women, in the best years of their lives, are educated not for purposes of their own, but for the external purposes of an alien social order. The university exists, it is said, simply to provide highly trained labor to the corporations, the government, or the knowledge factories. It is, therefore, an instrument of exploitation, a tool of the military-industrial complex or the one-dimensional consumer society. This sweeping proposition falls to the floor under its own weight. A sharp line cannot be drawn between the individual's "own purposes" and the purposes of the social order. A young man who wants to be a mathematician draws his own pleasure from that profession; the fact that it happens to be a useful profession does not mean that he has been dragooned into it against his will. To be socially useful is not to be exploited, and there is no society, existing or conceivable, which does not demand that its members make some contribution to the collective good.

The difference between one society and another lies in large part in the kinds of exception they make to this general rule, and in the flexibility and scope of their conceptions of social utility. From that point of view, contemporary American society is one of the more, rather than less, generous social orders. Of course, it is also true that in any society there are some jobs to which people have to be force-fitted. They may be useful jobs, but they satisfy no esthetic or moral craving of the individual who holds them. It is hard to see, however, how all such jobs can be eliminated—nor is it even plain that all people want to be stimulated by their work. Einstein said, towards the end of his life, that if he had to do it all over again, he would be a plumber. It was simple, self-respecting work, free from the constant pressure to produce and be "creative." But in any case, college and university education are the best avenues that exist in our society to the kind of work that combines personal commitment and social utility. Of all the groups in society to whom the word "exploitation" is least applicable from this point of view, college and university students would seem to be the most conspicuous.

Of course, the deeper assumption in the charge that higher education is "exploitative" is that it trains students for work which is frivolous or harmful, not useful. The basic purposes of the society are wicked, and its fundamental arrangements misconceived. But we need not examine that very large proposition here. True or not, it cannot be used to indict universities. For the universities are themselves the major centers in which that proposition, in its extreme or more moderate forms, flourishes. They shelter the teachers and students who express and propagate this view of American society. That in itself makes it impossible to denounce universities as unequivocal instruments of the status quo. At any rate, it makes it impossible if one respects facts.

And besides, what system of higher education in the world grants more freedom to students in their choice of studies than the one that now exists in the United States? What system has provided more room for individual variation, more flexibility in programs of study, more diversity in standards and style, more friendliness to eccentricities, rigid and unimaginative though many of its aspects may be? Assume the worst: say that the larger economic system is "exploitative"; say that it chains people to routines and purposes to which they have not consented and which they do not approve. Still, of all the parts of the existing social order, this indictment applies least of all to institutions of higher education. Very few of them fail to offer a viable alternative to the student who refuses to be co-opted into the system: he need merely study music, philosophy, and poetry, and join some protest group. And the chances are good that he will be offered a job by this "exploitative" system which will allow him to go on doing the same things after he has graduated.

Whatever may be wrong with American colleges and universities—and there is plenty—calling them "exploitative" is demagoguery. The war and the draft have changed the objective relation of students to their colleges, and have altered their inner feelings about the experience of education. These are real but circumscribable evils. Broadside attacks on the university system as such merely lead people away from effective action against these specific difficulties.

In sum, the case for student power cannot be presented as a case against tyranny and oppression. Nor can it be justified on the basis of fundamental student rights. It is highly desirable for a dozen reasons, I think, to give students a larger share of responsibility in the government of the institutions which they attend. But the issue is a matter of practical educational and political practice, not of the rights of man. And this distinction is important. To do something because it is desirable is not the same as to do it because it violates people's rights not to do it. The logic is different, and the consequences are different. Students are indeed members in good standing of a university community. But this community is a hierarchical human organization, based on the premise that some people know more than other people, and that the community cannot perform its tasks effectively unless these gradations in knowledge are recognized in its form of government. Allowing for certain qualifications, the rights which people acquire within this community are earned rights which they have to show that they merit.

This is not an abuse of "democracy." The right of a citizen of the larger society to vote just as the next man can, without regard to hierarchy, is based on the premise that, where the major policies of the State are concerned, where the nature of what is good for society is at issue, only extreme inadequacies, like illiteracy or a criminal record, are disqualifying. The basic reason for this view, according to the believer in democracy, is that there are no reasonably defensible general procedures by which the citizenry can be divided into the class of those who know enough to have an opinion worth counting or an interest worth expressing, and the class of those who don't. And, in addition, majority rule is accepted in democracies only because its range is restricted. Individuals have rights against majority rule, and all sorts of associations exist which are insulated against majority rule.

In contrast, while universities are democratic organizations in the sense that individuals have a broad array of personal rights within them, and that there is a play of opinion inside them which as a massive effect on their evolution, they are not democratic organizations in the sense that majority rule applies to them. For within a university there are acceptable procedures by which people can be graded in accordance with their competence, and grading people in this way is essential to the conduct of the university's special business. The egalitarian ideal does not apply across the board in universities any more than it does in any other field where *skill* is the essence of the issue. To suggest that it should apply is to make hash of the idea of learning. This involves, as the very language of the learned community suggests, the attainment of successive, and increasingly higher, *degrees* of competence. If there is a case to be made for student participation in the higher reaches of university government, it is a case that is not based upon *rights,* but upon considerations of good educational and administrative practice.

To examine this case, it is best to begin by looking at the status quo—the government of colleges and universities by trustees. Does the discussion we have just concluded imply that the present system is a good one? No; but it helps to put the examination of this system in perspective.

The case which is generally presented against trustee control of universities mixes truths with exaggerations. It is true that most trustees tend to be preoccupied with other matters than education, that they are inaccessible to teachers and students, and that a dispiriting number of them

118

have reached an age and station in life calculated to protect them against fresh ideas. It is not surprising, therefore, that professors and students are sparing in the confidence they lavish on trustees. The government of American universities by boards of trustees is not an example of government by the consent of the governed.

However, neither is it an example of tyranny. The powers of trustees are severely limited by custom and law, and by the realities of a university. In any well-established university, trustees normally leave educational decisions to the faculty. One of their primary educational functions, indeed, is simply to provide the educational community of the university—its students and faculty—with protective insulation. The trustees throw their mantle of influence and respectability around it, deflecting and absorbing criticisms and denunciations, and thus guarding the community's freedom. Indeed, it is doubtful that faculties and student bodies, in many parts of the country, could by themselves, and without the help of trustees, successfully defend their autonomy, even assuming that their economic problems could be solved. It is odd that trustees should be attacked as though their presence was in contravention of academic freedom. Their presence is usually a condition for it.

On the whole, indeed, trustees of private colleges and universities probably have a better record with regard to respecting the autonomy and freedom of faculty and students than do boards of regents, chosen by popular vote or appointed by a governor or other public official. Those who call for "democratic control" or "democratic participation" in the government of universities should reflect on the fact that there is a second version of the idea of "democratic control," not less acceptable than theirs, and perhaps somewhat easier to bring into being. If government of a university by private trustees is a form of despotism, why not turn over the government of the university to public control? This is certainly what is likely to happen if private funds are removed, and only tax revenues are available for supporting the institution. Yet most of the evidence suggests that when the general public, through its political processes, exercises control, the autonomy of the faculty and students tends to be put under greater pressure than when private trustees are in control. When a legislature votes the budget, it is usually much more insistent on knowing why Professor X, the mathematician, is sounding off on the glories of Cuba, or how that ragged crowd of students who took over the Administration Hall could ever have slipped through a decent admissions procedure.

The comparison between the record of boards of trustees and that of boards of regents should not, of course, be pushed too hard. In most parts of the United States, public higher education is not now significantly different from private education with respect to the academic freedoms it provides. What is different, however, is the story behind that equal academic freedom. The presidents of public universities generally have to conduct a

119

much severer campaign of public education, and spend a good deal more of their time defending the rights of individuals, than do the heads of large private institutions. If there were no private institutions, this task might well be even more difficult. The private institutions help set the standards. The government of some universities by private trustees is a general condition for maintaining the variety and independence of American education at large.

Still, whether we are discussing boards of trustees or boards of regents, it can be asked whether this form of government is the best form for a college or university. Trustees (or regents) do make educational decisions, even if most of these are only indirect. They allocate resources, do more for one field of learning than for another, and make arrangements affecting the relation of the university to the larger society which bear on the daily lives of teachers and students. Would it not be better if trustees continued to do their work of finding the money, but surrendered the other powers they exercise to the people who really constitute the university—namely, its students and teachers? Obviously, it is doubtful that many trustees would accept this proposal that they should supply the money but keep quiet about the way it is used. Just to see where the argument goes, however, let us imagine that trustees have a capacity for self-immolation not conspicuous in most human beings. Would it be a good thing for them to retire from the scene?

Not entirely. They are the buffers of the university against external pressures. As we have seen, an educational institution requires such protection. Most organizations, furthermore, benefit from having a lay group of critics with deep commitments to them, who are nevertheless not part of their daily operations. In addition, since universities must maintain relations with the surrounding society, they require people on their board of governors who have interests and experience in that society. And it is always well to remember that, though education, like the law, is in part a professional business, it is also everybody's business. If students have a stake in what happens to them, by the same token, so do their parents and so do lay members of the community. In courts of law, juries are not composed of professional lawyers. On the university scene, the outsider, though he should not have as decisive a place as a juror has, also deserves to be represented.

In part, this function is served by the activities of alumni, and by the presence of alumni on most boards of trustees, and, in principle, it could be served by restricting the "outside" membership on such boards only to alumni. But only in part. Alumni bodies are immensely varied. The main source of private funds for some universities is the alumni, but this is not true for others. And alumni represent only one relevant point of view. There are other "outside" constituencies which a university should serve, and which should be represented on its governing board. In general, the needs of most universities justify the proposition that they should be ruled,

120

at least in part, by people who are not active members of them, including people who have not studied at them.

Yet these same considerations call for change in the composition of most boards of trustees. They call, equally clearly, for changes in the manner in which they communicate with the communities they govern. Boards of trustees ought to have more younger people on them, and poorer people. They ought to have recent graduates, and not only older ones. They ought to have people who have not yet arrived, and not only those swollen with success. The surrounding neighborhood should, if possible, be represented. That is not always easy to arrange because there are so often disagreements about who is "representative" of whom. But if it can be done without creating quarrels that did not exist before, then it should be done. And students and faculty members should either be represented on the board, or should be assured of regular consultation with it.

The case for such changes is not open and shut. Faculties lose some of their cherished independence if they share with trustees the burdens of budget-making, real estate deals, and community politics. The extension of university self-government almost certainly involves the proliferation of still more of the committees which are the bane of many professors' lives; there can come a day when professors—and students on their committees—will curse the people who demanded "democracy" in the university, and yearn for the "despotism" under which they once suffered. Almost certainly, self-government in a university is not likely to be an enterprise in which all will participate. It should not be. A large number of professors are likely to think, and with reason, that they have other and better things to do. A large number of students may have the same idea.

But for those who want to participate, there should be an opportunity to do so. There are clear advantages to giving members of a faculty the assurance that they are represented in the decision-making procedures of their institution. The sense of distance from the institution's center has had at least something to do with the increasing mobility of professors, their lack of interest in the collective business of their institution, and their orientation towards professional organizations or community problems off the campus. The inaccessibility or uncommunicativeness of administrators is the single largest cause of declining morale in a college or university. The only thing worse, perhaps, is an excessively accessible and communicative administrator who is a simpleton. How to guarantee faculty communication with administrators and trustees—whether this should be done by guaranteeing faculty representation on the board of trustees or by other means —is a question to which answers will vary because situations are variable. But it is difficult to argue against the proposition that trustees and faculty should be in continuing communication, and that this has not been the normal pattern.

The participation of students in the supreme governing bodies of a uni-

121

versity raises issues that are equally subtle. Students are inexperienced. They are present on a campus for only a short period, and could serve on committees and boards for only a shorter period. It takes time, on most boards and committees, before new members learn enough to become genuinely useful. Student generations change in their styles and opinions, furthermore, and sometimes very quickly. Students, therefore, bring an element of discontinuity, a shortened perspective and sometimes a short fuse, into the consideration of matters of policy. In educational institutions particularly, continuity of perspective and some sense of the time-dimension are essential.

Finally, student representation on the permanent governing bodies of a university poses a complex problem both practically and theoretically. How do we arrange this "representation" so that it is representative? In a liberal-arts college the problem is manageable. But in a university, with its scores of schools and faculties and its variegated student-body, this is considerably easier to talk about in the abstract than to produce in the concrete. Nothing could do greater and quicker harm to the cause of "student power" than the complaint that the students officially representing their fellows are not really representative of them.

In sum, the idea of student membership on boards of trustees raises as many problems as it seems to solve. Nevertheless, the idea is worth experimentation, even though the number of students who belong to a board, or who sit with it when certain issues are discussed, should probably be small. And there is little question, apart from the formalities of representation on a board of trustees, that machinery for regular face-to-face meetings between students and trustees is desirable. Discontinuity in policy is dangerous, but so is automatic, thoughtless continuity. The long view is estimable, but impatience is useful too. And if inexperience is a handicap, so is experience: it dulls one to novelty. Trustees could learn from students things they will never learn from administrators or other trustees.

In the end, we are discussing not matters of right and justice, but matters of political wisdom. Trustees will not know what they should know unless they mix with the people who can tell them. The community they govern will not understand why the trustees have made the decisions they have, and will not have a confidence in these decisions, unless it has its own trusted emissaries to keep it in touch with the board. Faulty communication is the heart of the political problem in the American universities that are today having trouble. Demands for "student power" and "faculty power," so interpreted, are more than justifiable.

One more word, however, is in order. The discussion we have just concluded turns on the distinction between students' *right* to be represented in the government of a college or university, and the desirability, for other reasons, of giving students closer access to the university's important decision-making procedures. The argument has been an argument from desir-

122

bility and not from rights. But this should not be interpreted as meaning that, within a university, students have no rights. They have rights as citizens of the larger society, which they do not lose when they become members of a higher educational institution, and they also have rights that derive from their special status as students.

The term "power," when used in political contexts, has three levels of meaning. At the highest level, it can mean participation in the actual business of government. At a somewhat more restricted level, it can mean access to the people in authority so that one can advance one's own ideas or interests. At the most elementary level, it means that one possesses certain rights as against those who govern, and that one has what it takes to protect these rights. The most elementary meaning of "student power" is that students have such rights. As citizens, they have rights of free speech and association, and are free to exercise them, subject only to the impact on the rights of others. Similarly, students have the right to petition for redress of grievances; the right to organize legal political actions; the right to live their own lives when off the campus, subject only to the laws and the risks of the larger society. They also have a right, it seems to me, which is increasingly important today, and is too often violated: this is the right to control the use of their academic records.

As for the special rights which inhere in their status as students, they have, for example, the right to invite speakers of their own choice to address their organizations, and to ask the university to provide the facilities required. So far as university authorities are concerned, this is not a matter of educational discretion, but of recognizing a valid claim. Students are captive audiences, forced to hear the opinions of their professors. Their right to free inquiry should imply that they have a right to seek alternative points of view. Other rights of the same kind—for example, the right to due process in disciplinary proceedings when they so request also belong to them. These rights, as a day-to-day matter, are as important to students as the enhancement of their power over the decision-making functions of a university.

All or most of these rights are recognized, however, in all or most colleges and universities in the country. The live question now is not whether students should have them. It is how far they go. And that brings up the question of the tactics that have been employed at Columbia and many other institutions, ostensibly in the pursuit of student rights.

FOR AND AGAINST STUDENT PARTICIPATION

EARL J. McGRATH

RATIONALE FOR STUDENT PARTICIPATION

What specific reasons can be advanced for giving students a formal role in academic government? The most compelling rests on the generally accepted political proposition that in free societies all those affected by a social policy have an inalienable right to a voice in it its formulation. In this sense, students are today not adequately free. Only through emancipation from the institutional restrictions imposed by others, and by full participation in academic deliberative and legislative processes, can they gain the status of self-determining individuals. Assured of these rights, they could play a not insignificant role in altering the policies and practices which they consider offensive to free men.

Institutional Professions and Actions

Students today, perhaps more clearly than any earlier generation, perceive the arresting contrasts between the democratic views of the members of the academic guild on domestic and international issues and the restricted human relationships they condone in the society of learning. With unprecedented awareness this generation of youth grasps the crucial relationship between education and human destiny. They understand that the amount and kind of education one receives largely determines his social status, his economic well-being, and the effectiveness of his participation in the life of his time. Aside from these private concerns, students recognize that universal and effective education is the *sine qua non* of our domestic well-being and our position among the nations. Accepting this momentous view of education generally proclaimed by the members of the academic establishment, they wonder why the microcosm of learning should not reflect the social philosophy and political practices of the larger society of which it is such an important part. If, as they are told, education is of such fateful significance, and if they are to be the recipients of its benefits, they are understandably asking why they do not have a recognized voice in determing its character and quality.

The Sophistication of Students Today

Another reason for students' involvement in governance relates to the concerns and motivations of youth today. Students' preoccupations suggest that they could be more thoughtfully effective than their predecessors in taking part in the reform of higher education. In contrast to earlier generations, today's students have a more serious and informed interest in the social, economic, racial, political, and international problems of their age. They have also become sensitively conscious of the potential therapeutic value of education in curing the ills of an ailing humanity. Unlike the teachers and parents of an earlier time, those of the seventies cannot rightly complain about the social, political, or intellectual apathy of most college and university students. In fact, the current complaint is not about lethargy, but the reverse, activism! Students are now concerned about the relationship (or the lack of it) between the exercises of the classroom, the library, and the laboratory, on the one hand, and their own existence and the conditions of life generally, on the other. Socially conscious as they now are, it is not surprising that the personal and social goals of students move them to be seriously dissatisfied with the unrepresentativeness of academic bodies and with the inadequacy of decision-making processes and the elephantine cumbersomeness of legislative action in colleges and universities. In this unprecedented intellectual concern and idealistic commitment, there is an immense potential for the thoughtful reconstruction of higher education and of American society.

Students Should Be Educated
for Democratic Living

A third justification for student participation in academic government stems from ubiquitously declared goals of American institutions of higher education. Educators, particularly social philosophers, consider the preparation of youth for the exacting responsibilities of citizenship in an increasingly complex democratic society to be one of the most important purposes of colleges and universities. Yet faculty members establish, or at least unwittingly acquiesce in, practices which deny students the right to learn about, and to become skilled in the exercise of, these civic responsibilities. Examples of such contrasts in profession and practice are easy to find. Consider the selection of the outside speakers who address students in a campus lecture series. Administrators and faculty committees make prohibitive decisions without consulting, or in direct violation of, student opinion concerning the persons they wish to hear discuss the issues which they consider vital. Similarly, faculties or trustees, as in some California institutions, have abridged the students' opportunity to receive instruction from persons who are unable to meet the academic establishment's inflexible qualifying standards, but who students consider especially fitted to discuss important problems of the day. Students believe that if they had a proper role in academic government, an important dimension would be added to their education and an indispensable element to their preparation for effective citizenship.

Students Could Help Improve Higher Education

Fourth among the reasons for student participation in the deliberation of faculty bodies is that students could accelerate the correction of patent deficiencies in present curricular offerings. Even admitting the ambiguity and misunderstanding which now envelop the word "relevant," it is fair to say that many courses which students are now required to pursue do not prepare them very well to come to grips with the major problems of their personal and public lives. For a quarter of a century a small group of highly respected educators, like Robert M. Hutchins at the University of Chicago and James B. Conant at Harvard University, recognized that much college instruction merely prepares the student for futher instruction and that only in the most derivative and remote sense can such teaching be considered to relate to life beyond the classroom walls. This fragmentation, specialization, and conceptualization of learning does not invalidate its usefulness for the minority of students who pursue it for vocational ends as, for example, candidates for the Ph.D. degree, but it does cause inexcusable gaps in the education of the larger majority. Since students far more than any other persons are where educational action is—in the classroom— they are perforce better informed about educational substance and processes. The significance of higher education in the life of the average educated American would doubtless be increased if students sat on committees which determine the character and content of instruction.

Moreover, if students enjoyed membership in influential faculty committees, they might help in restoring some sense of unity and meaning to the infinitely varied course complexes which now constitute individual degree programs. The resolution of today's social, economic, racial, and philosophic issues, and the related human problems, requires that citizens have a more comprehensive knowledge and greater range of intellectual skills than undergraduate education now typically provides. The abject conditions of the poor, the hungry, the sick, and the ignorant and the means of their alleviation cannot be understood by "taking" a single course in economics, sociology, political science, or any other subject. Even when some portion of the content of such courses bear directly on the current circumstances of life, the inherent logic of a single discipline

126

tends to limit the range of its application. Consider one example of the need for breadth of knowledge and skills in the intelligent solution of pressing problems in American culture. The social determinants of the life of the disadvantaged, and the means of their amelioration, must be approached from the position of not one or two disciplines, but from those of economics, psychology, penology, medicine, genetics, and political science, as well as other branches of learning. As students juxtapose their learning experiences in the classroom with the events in the world outside, they feel that their education is not sufficiently broad and relevant to the personal and social decisions their generation will be called upon to make if the human condition is to be improved. Rightly or wrongly, students believe that if they were given a voice in academic bodies, they could be helpful in bringing instruction closer not only to their own interests but to the conditions of modern life generally.

The Abolition of the Doctrine of
In Loco Parentis

A fifth justification for student involvement concerns the general conditions, and the style, of life in the academic community. American institutions of higher education, unlike most of their European counterparts, have historically assumed the responsibility of acting on behalf of parents while their sons or daughters are in residence. Under the doctrine of *in loco parentis* institutions have regulated the lives of students and imposed the most objectionably repressive measures to govern their personal conduct. In addition to laying down scholastic regulations custodial supervision has determined the kinds of personal associations students could have, their right to leave the campus, their recreational activities, and a host of other private matters.

Many, even those who do not press for student representation in other areas of policy-making, feel that in respect to their personal lives institutions still improperly treat students like irresponsible children rather than like maturing adults. The unrealistic and futile character of this pseudo-parental attitude is well illustrated in the comment of a coed in a college which includes work experience as one of the requirements for a degree. She observed that it was ridiculous to require a man to leave her dormitory room at eleven o'clock when during the previous six months she had entertained whom she pleased when she pleased and how she pleased in her South Chicago apartment. During the past several years, students have found these parietal regulations more irritating than any other rules. The choosing of human associations and the shaping of a private life, so long as these personal decisions do not restrict the freedom of others, ought to be experiences which contribute to the achievement of mature adult conduct. Since decision-making in respect to personal conduct is as essential a part of education as participation in the determination of more strictly

127

academic policies, students can with equal propriety claim membership in academic bodies which make parietal rules.

The Improvement of Instruction

The sixth, and perhaps the most persuasive, argument for student participation in academic government rests on the special and sometimes unique information students possess about the teaching-learning situation. Students have certain experiences which qualify them to make more reliable judgments than their associates among the trustees, administrators, or faculty members. These experiences concern matters related to, but quite different from, the content of courses or the substantive relationships among them discussed earlier. Students are peculiarly situated to make judgments concerning the faculty member's performance in discharging his responsibilities in the classroom. Since custom, if not ethics, prevents all others from viewing the instructional situation, students are the only group capable of gathering the relevant facts. Only they can day by day actually observe the practitioner's fulfillment of his professional obligations—his knowledge of his subject, his preparation for the presentation of specific assignments, his attitude toward and availability to students who may need additional help, and his conscientiousness in seeing that research and consulting do not interfere with his teaching obligations.

It is generally agreed that the large increase in the number of students in recent years has interfered with the carrying out of some traditional teaching activities. That too many teachers have too many students is generally recognized, and the consequent neglect of some students under present circumstances is unavoidable. But the allowance of outside professional activities to interfere with the work of the classroom has been less widely recognized, or at least less publicized. Yet the practice of neglecting some of the traditional responsibilities of college teaching has become epidemic. Since the end of World War II it has been a problem much exacerbated by the availability to an increasing proportion of faculty members of other types of preferred professional activities—doing research, writing learned articles, and advising corporations and the government. Some members of the profession should doubtless be permitted, indeed encouraged, to devote themselves exclusively to such non-teaching responsibilities, while others give their undivided efforts to teaching. Except in such recognized cases, however, students have a right to expect presumptive teachers to teach. If students, often the sole possessors of relevant information, were given an officially recognized role in evaluating individual faculty members on established criteria of acceptable teaching performance, they might assist in the correction of the present inadequacies in teaching.

Although the case can easily be made for a role for students in the reform of teaching, it is significant that of all the policy-making bodies to which students have gained access, the committee on faculty selection, promotion, and tenure falls near the bottom of the list. Only 4.7 percent of the

128

875 reporting institutions have admitted students to committees on faculty appointment, promotion, and tenure, and in only 3.3 percent do they vote. Yet it is the faculty members who provide (or do not provide) effective instruction. When compared to the much larger percentages of membership in other committees, these figures seem to justify the inference that the profession more often favors student involvement in committees which set other policies than those which pass judgment on the effectiveness of its own membership.

Students are beginning to recognize that the character and quality of their education will be determined not so much by the kinds of persons who occupy trusteeships or administrative offices, but by the qualifications, the interests, the attitudes, and the dedication of the men and women they meet in the classroom. Moreover, they are coming to realize that the kinds of teachers they have will to a considerable extent be determined by the role students play in their selection. With students on no more than 4.7 percent of committees on faculty selection, promotion, and tenure, their progress toward gaining this kind of influence is clearly negligible. It has often been said that the quality of education a particular institution offers is determined by the kinds of faculty members who serve it. Since students increasingly recognize this fact of academic life, and since they feel that they have constructive criticisms to make with respect to their education, they believe that they ought to have a voice in selecting staff members and evaluating their professional performance.

OBJECTIONS TO STUDENT PARTICIPATION

The foregoing arguments in favor of the involvement of students in academic government, as persuasive as they are to some, leave others unconvinced. Many informed and sincere persons firmly believe that if students gain an authentic voice in academic government, the ends of higher education will at best be confused, and at worst subverted. Their reasons for taking this position deserve thoughtful consideration.

Students Will Dominate the Academic Society

The critics most serious question on student participation has to do with the power structure within the academic polity. The locus of power in colleges and universities is a complicated and somewhat obscure subject, which an analysis of the related legal documents is more likely to obfuscate than to illuminate. Although the cure of the maladies which now afflict the academic organism requires a discriminating diagnosis of the political forces now at work, a proper examination of this matter lies beyond the scope of the present discussion. Nevertheless, until such a review has been made, one aspect of the power structure must be given attention in any consideration of the objections to student participation.

Some opponents contend that the admission of students to important academic bodies would so alter the balance of power within them that, in fact, virtual control would shift from the board, the administration, and the faculty to the students. The antagonists to student participation do not usually spell out the theoretical results of such a realignment of control, but they do point to their concrete mainfestations in some of the recent "neo-negotiable" demands of activists. They show that these ultimata have included virtually the full range of institutional policies and practices. Student groups have made efforts (sometimes successfully) to eliminate individual courses and indeed whole curricula which they found objectionable and to introduce others they favored. They have caused teachers and administrators of whom for one reason or another they disapproved to be removed and other acceptable substitutes to be appointed. They have been able to halt the erection of some buildings and to initiate the construction of others. They have caused the radical revision of admission standards and the inauguration of elaborate new advisory systems. The evidence is conclusive that students have already effected many basic changes in American higher education. And most of these results have been accomplished without official status. Witnessing all that students have achieved with the sanction of neither law nor custom, those who oppose their participation fear the more radical changes which authentic involvement might be expected to bring.

The Immaturity of Students

A second objection to student involvement concerns their youth and limited life experience. Critics consider the behavior of today's students, especially undergraduates, at times capricious and frivolous, at other times inflexible and dogmatic—in a word, immature. A judicious observer will not overlook the fact that these judgments rest largely on the behavior of students in those institutions whose turbulence has recently been the center of national attention. On these campuses many have acted with little or no regard for conventional codes of behavior. They have unconscionably violated the rights of other members of the community and capriciously established their own value system for the appraisal of human conduct. They have created their own dogmas, sometimes more unyielding than those they have been designed to replace. They have failed to display the kind of balanced judgment which is supposed to characterize the cultivated mind. In brief, however valid the students' animadversions against the academic establishment may be, critics believe that youth's efforts at reform have often lacked the intellectual and emotional restraint associated with maturity. Defenders of students say that this is too much to expect from young people in their late teens or early twenties. The opposition promptly agrees with this judgment and cites it as their primary reason for not giving students a decisive role in academic government.

The Brief Involvement of Students

In the matter of student participation the members of the profession voice a third reservation. They point out that most students, especially the numerous undergraduates, spend only four years in any one institution, and many spend only a year or two. Under these circumstances some of the more permanent staff members question whether even the most earnest students can acquire the perspective and the commitment essential to sound judgment on long-term policies. These senior professionals doubt not only that students can deal prudently with the issues and problems related to the destiny of a college or university, but that they can deal wisely with the personal well-being of the large company who have cast their lot with it. A typically brief association, it is contended, will predispose students to be interested primarily in policies of immediate benefit to themselves.

Critics cite an increase in tuition fees as an example of conflict between immediate personal and more permanent institutional values. To prevent a rise in the cost of their education, students have demonstrated against the imposition of higher fees. Yet a balanced concern for the long-term quality of the faculty and the general maintenance of standards might at a particular time require acceptance of such an action. Similarly, the adoption of fashionable but exotic curricular proposals may satisfy the passing fancy of short-term residents, but may not be in the best interest of institutional stability and economic soundness. The critics buttress their view by pointing out that students' indifference to long-run institutional welfare is confirmed by the shallow and transient concern of alumni, whose devotion to alma mater, once they have gained the degree, rapidly evaporates. Many faculty members, some of whom give a whole professional life to a particular institution, contend that neither their own nor the institution's welfare should be placed in the hands of those with such ephemeral commitments. That this view does not spring from a prejudice against students is proven by the fact that it has been applied to young faculty members in the lower ranks, who, because of their probable short service, are denied faculty status. The argument based on the shortness of institutional affiliation is one which advocates of student participation have yet to deal with adequately.

Ignorance of Professional Values

A fourth objection to a larger role for students in academic government is related to, but differs basically from, the shortness of the students' institutional affiliation. It is also related to maturity but specifically concerns one of its components, specialized abilities, and embraces the rich complement of comprehensive knowledge and special skills that is involved in the broad practice of a profession. The components of understanding, esoteric knowledge, and seasoned judgment that characterize the expert and confident practitioner of any profession are acquired slowly. Yet, to an extraordinary degree, those who have risen to the highest pinnacle of professional success have exhibited these essential and unique qualities. One

131

need only mention such names as Charles W. Eliot, William James, Sir William Osler, and Joseph Storey to prove the point that genuine professionalism comprises not only a complex of specialized knowledge and skill, but a keen awareness of the meaning of a calling in relation to the larger human enterprise.

Now, to be sure, not all members of a profession such as teaching, even those with senior status, achieve the fullness of knowledge and the ripeness of judgment characteristic of its examplars. All do, however, grow in these respects as they practice their craft. This is especially true of college and university faculty members whose profession not only permits, but requires, the evaluation of prospective policies within a larger social context. If the forward motion of the academic enterprise is slow, it is in part because its members are sensitive to the values they have a moral responsibility to protect and preserve. Knowing as they do how priceless and yet how tenuous are the privileges of academic life, faculty members are loath to share responsibility for their preservation with the uninitiated. They object, therefore, to enfranchising students in regard to matters with which they can at best be uninformedly sympathetic and at worst callously indifferent.

Interference with Study and
Gainful Employment

A fifth objection to student participation comes from some educators who oppose it not in principle, but for the practical reason that in the nature of things students cannot give the time necessary for a faithful discharge of their responsibilities. Those critics who have had the experience of meeting with committees for several hours a week sometimes for a full academic year or more know what a distractive burden such activities can be. They doubt whether even the ablest student could devote the required large proportion of his out-of-class time to committee work without adversely affecting his educational progress. The experience of entirely sympathetic academic administrators here and in Canada where students have sat on faculty committees supports this *a priori* conclusion. Some students have offered similar testimony either by direct statement or by their increasing absence from meetings as the growing burden of work has interfered with their academic obligations. Moreover, as students realize the weight of the responsibilities imposed by their obligation to report what has transpired in committee to their constituency, the whole student body, and to seek a consensus on at least the most important issues under discussion, they find themselves in a serious moral conflict. They have to choose whether they will neglect their studies at great personal sacrifice or neglect their representational obligations at the expense of their fellow students. Many unbiased persons believe that until some way is found out of this dilemma, it is delusive and futile to advocate or accept student representation in academic policy-making bodies.

132

STUDENT PARTICIPATION IN CURRICULUM PLANNING AND EVALUATION

CARL SLATER, M.D.

STUDENTS SHOULD BE FORMAL participants in the decision-making related to curriculum planning in all medical schools. The most basic reason is given by John Gardner[1] in his book, *Self-Renewal: The Individual and the Innovative Society:* "Innovation and renewal within an organization require multiple points of initiative and decision-making with constant attention to goals." Clearly, the medical school is an organization in need of ongoing innovation and renewal, and the application of Gardner's principle to the medical school requires curriculum planning which involves the contributions of many groups, including students.

The present proliferation of reports and conferences on medical education reflects the need for changes. Medical schools, which have become largely scientific enterprises, should develop greater responsiveness to society. Large numbers of medical students have first-hand experience to contribute to this effort, much of which they have gained in the social movements of the past five years: the civil rights struggle, the Vietnam war protest, and the reforms in the universities. Both Funkenstein[2] and Keniston[3] emphasize the need to draw on rather than to ignore this experience; it can be the students' unique contribution to the process of curriculum innovation. Ebert[4] states, ". . . the students will provide the necessary prod to a conservative profession and a conservative educational process." Unfor-

---

[1]J.W. Gardner, *Self-Renewal: The Individual and the Innovative Society* (New York: Harper and Row, 1963).

[2]D.H. Funkenstein, "The Learning and Personal Development of Medical Students and the Recent Changes in Universities and Medical Schools," *Journal of Medical Education,* Vol. 43 (1968), pp. 883-897.

[3]K. Keniston, "The Medical Student," *New Physicians,* Vol. 17 (1968), pp. 226-231.

[4]R.H. Ebert, "Medical Care: Reform the System!" *Harvard Today* (Spring, 1968), pp. 11-16.

Reprinted from the Journal of Medical Education, *Vol. 44 (August, 1969), pp. 675-678, with permission of the Association of American Medical Colleges and the author.*

tunately, students are not involved effectively in curriculum innovation (or planning for the future) in the vast majority of medical schools; they only participate formally in curriculum evaluation (or assessment of the past). The analysis of two questionnaires, one administered by the Student American Medical Association (SAMA) and the other distributed jointly by SAMA and the Association of American Medical Colleges' Group on Student Affairs (GSA), documents this fact.

To obtain data on the extent and success of student involvement, the first questionnaire was sent to all SAMA chapter presidents and the second to each medical school's administrative officer with primary responsibility for student affairs. Fixty-six of the questionnaires sent to students were returned and 95 student affairs officers responded. With respect to the extent of participation, 75 of the latter group reported some student involvement in planning and 90 some involvement in evaluation, but only 36 indicated that there was formal student representation on faculty committees in their schools. The number of student responses in each of these categories was 39, 51, and 29, respectively. Clearly, the extent of formal student involvement is limited.

The reasons that the student affairs officers gave for not including a formal student representative on faculty committees are shown in Table 1.

TABLE 1
REASONS GIVEN BY STUDENT AFFAIRS OFFICERS FOR NOT HAVING
FORMAL STUDENT REPRESENTATION ON FACULTY COMMITTEES

Comment	No. of Schools
No reason why not	12
Does not appear necessary	5
Feel that students are not sophisticated enough to make useful suggestions	4
Students would inhibit frank discussion	3
Policy is faculty responsibility	3
Student opinion more effective without personal representative	3
Too small a school	3
Not convinced of benefits	3
Faculty opposition	3
Based on old administrative decision	2
No student push for such	2
No reply*	52
Total	95

*Thirty-six did not answer the question because students were formally represented on faculty committees.

---

*Delivered to the Group on Student Affairs at the 79th Annual Meeting of the Association of American Medical Colleges, Houston, Texas, November 1, 1968.

134

The success of student participation was determined by asking each of the student affairs officers to cite an example of a contribution that the students had made to curricular change in his school. In the analysis of the responses, the cited student contributions were assigned to one of two categories: Category 1 (modification) included those citations that related to relatively minor changes in existing curricular structure, including such areas as course organization, scheduling, examination, and grading policies. Category 2 (innovation) included contributions to the establishment of new courses, multitrack curricula, large-scale elective programs, attempts to improve the school's basic educational environment, and the like. The results of this analysis are presented in Table 2. Clearly, most student contributions were in the modification category. This impression is further substantiated by the student curriculum reports that the student affairs officers returned with their questionnaires. A review of the reports revealed a paucity of innovative thinking and a preoccupation with the "how" of medical education. If curriculum innovation is one of the areas for unique contributions by students, their efforts to date can only be called modestly successful.

Apparently, students have had limited success for one reason: the optimal mechanisms for student participation in curriculum innovation have not been clearly understood or implemented. One indication of that is that students are not formally involved in the decision-making process in over half of the medical schools. To illuminate these statements the data shown in Table 2 have been arranged so as to relate the results of student contri-

TABLE 2

MECHANISMS OF PARTICIPATION CITED BY STUDENT AFFAIRS OFFICERS

	No. of Schools	Student Contributions to Change			
		Category 1 (Modification)	Category 2 (Innovation)	Too Early to Determine	No Reply
Student representatives on faculty committees					
Elected	23	18	0	5	0
Appointed	9	0	2	3	4
No reply	4	0	0	0	4
Total	36	18	2	8	8
Student curriculum committees which meet with faculty committees					
Elected	13	5	2	5	1
Voluntary	4*	1	4	0	0
Total	17	6	6	5	1

*One school in both categories.

butions to the means for achieving them. It appears that different mechanisms are responsible for qualitatively different results. Student representatives on faculty committees contribute largely to the modification of present curricula. In contrast, separate student curriculum committees meeting with faculty committees have contributed equally to innovation (6 schools) and to modification (6 schools). Similarly, there is some indication that elected students are more concerned with modification (23 modifiers versus 2 innovators) and volunteer or appointed students are more likely to contribute innovations (6 innovators versus 1 modifier). The apparent lesson is that independent student committees have the most to offer to curriculum innovation.

Recommendations

Several recommendations are implicit from this discussion:

1. Students offer two unique experience areas which are important in curriculum planning: (a) They are the ones experiencing the educational process. This position gives them a chance to spot sources of irritation and to see the entire spectrum of the curriculum. (b) From their increased exposure to society and its medical problems through summer projects and the like they bring an enhanced awareness of the needs of physicians who will in the future practice medicine in the community.

2. Their particular contributions can be made to curriculum planning most effectively through student curriculum committees working with faculty curriculum committees. Modifying functions may be carried out adequately by elected student representatives, but innovative functions should involve voluntary student curriculum committees that delegate members to meet with faculty committees. In either case, selected students should be full voting members of all faculty curriculum committees. Otherwise, they and the faculty may continue to feel that they are only "playing a game."

The students, through the SAMA Committee on Medical Education, have begun to implement these recommendations in several ways:

1. An *Ad Hoc* Committee for Communication on Medical Education has been established. This Committee includes one representative, with an expressed interest in medical education, from every medical school in the United States. The purpose of this Committee is to collect and distribute information on medical education. Regular mailings go to each member with duplicates to each dean.

2. A Student Conference on Medical Education, jointly sponsored by SAMA, AMA, and AAMC, was held in February, 1969[5]. The Conference

---

[5] J.E. Chapman, "Student Input in Medical Education: A Medical Educator's Report," *Journal of Medical Education,* Vol. 44 (1969), pp. 542-545; B. Fagel, D. Schumacher and C. Slater, "Student Input in Medical Education: A Student View," *Journal of Medical Education,* Vol. 44 (1969), pp. 545-547.

included in its objectives the improvement of both the modifying and the innovative contributions of medical students.

3. A Commission on Medical Education has been formed by SAMA to achieve a synthesis of the ideas of the groups involved in medical education.

At each medical school, the dean and student affairs officer can implement these recommendations by encouraging faculty discussion, offering administrative support to the school's representative on the *Ad Hoc* Committee, and providing financial aid for appropriate students to attend conferences on medical education. In this way effective mechanisms for student participation in curriculum planning and evaluation can be developed, and John Gardner's goal of continuous self-renewal may be realized.

Acknowledgments

The author acknowledges the assistance of Dr. John Githens, Chairman of the GSA Committee on Communication with Student Organizations, Dr. Davis Johnson, Director of the AAMC Division of Student Affairs, and the student affairs officers for help in the collection of data; Robert Graham, Chairman, SAMA Commission on Medical Education, for helping to analyze the data; and the fellows and staff of the University of Illinois Center for the Study of Medical Education for assistance in the preparation of this report.

STUDENT PARTICIPATION IN UNIVERSITY EDUCATIONAL DECISION MAKING

FRED N. KERLINGER

IN THEIR ZEAL to participate in the educational process, students are demanding more and more of university administrators and faculties. This zeal is commendable. More important, it can have educationally desirable outcomes. But if permitted to go as far as many students seem to want it to go, its outcomes can also be highly undesirable. It can damage professorial rights and responsibilities. It can seriously harm the students' education. It can even change the purposes of the university.

The arguments used by students and those faculty who support student participation in educational decision making are highly appealing. It is said that university professors and administrators should democratically practice what they preach and give those most affected by educational decision making a real participatory role in the decision-making process. Democracy demands participation of all in decision making, it is said. This means that faculty and students should work together and have equal say in creating policy. The remote, cold, and authoritarian establishment should be radically altered, if not destroyed, and a truly democratic institution created. In short, the university should be truly democratized.

The purpose of this paper is to examine and analyze the educational decision-making function in the university and to indicate the implications and possible consequences of granting student demands to participate in decision making. By "participation in decision making" is meant that students will have equal rights with faculty to debate and vote on educational policy matters. Let us first look at the sources of university educational decision making.

EDUCATIONAL POLICY AND FACULTY DECISION MAKING

Educational policy making is, or should be, a faculty function. Only the faculty of a university is qualified to decide the structure and content of

Reprinted from the Teachers College Record, *Vol. 70, No. 1 (October, 1968), pp. 45-51, with permission of the Teachers College Record and the author.*

courses of instruction, instructional programs and curricula, and means and methods of teaching. Students can and should criticize existing policy and practice and suggest changes. But only the faculty members of institutions of higher learning—professionals specially trained to help further the basic goals of the university: the advancement of knowledge and the transmission of knowledge, or inquiry and teaching—can and should decide upon policies, practices, and changes.

Students do not seem to understand that educational decision making must rest with the faculty. They seem to think that programs, curricula, and courses of study are the result of some sort of fiat, perhaps administrative, perhaps not. This fuzzy conception of where decision responsibility lies helps to feed the wish to participate, democratically and equally, in the educational decision-making process. It feeds the wish, quite probably, because the university administration is covertly seen as the source of university power. Students, in their rebellion against the establishment, want some of this power. In other words, partly because of an often correct perception of where university general power lies but an incorrect perception of the legitimate source of educational decision making, students demand participation in such decision making.

CRITERIA OF DECISION MAKING

Few professors would deny students the right somehow to participate in university decision making or would deny the educational and personal value of such participation. The question is: In what aspects of decision making should students participate? The answer hinges on three principles, or criteria, that are expressed by the words legitimacy, competence, and responsibility. *Legitimacy* of decision making means the right, by law, policy, or obligation, to make decisions in a specified area. *Competence* in decision making means that an individual has the requisite knowledge and background that make it possible for him to participate intelligently and rationally in decisions about the area requiring the knowledge and background. *Responsibility* means that the individual making a decision has to be accountable for the implications and consequences of the decision. He has to live with its aftermath. Moreover, he has to answer to others for the decision and its outcomes. It is said that he is "held to account" for his actions. He can, in short, lose status, influence, and position as a consequence of bad decision making.

If we apply these three principles or criteria to student participation in university decision making, the major part of the question asked earlier can be answered. Students should participate in making decisions on those matters that are legitimate to student concerns and that do not infringe on the legitimacy of others. They should participate in decision making on those matters for which they have competence and not on those matters for which

139

they lack competence. Finally, they should participate in decision making only on those matters for which they can be held responsible. There are a number of areas of university and student life that are appropriate for student decision making. Student discipline, living conditions and arrangements, student publications, and student social affairs are examples.

Matters of actual educational moment, on the other hand, are not appropriate for student decision making. These include educational program, curriculum, course structure and content, admission requirements, and the like. The policies behind these matters are the concern only of the faculty. This is because students do not satisfy and cannot satisfy the three decision-making criteria, as far as these matters are concerned. First, take legitimacy. Faculty determination of educational matters is university policy in most universities. The only legitimate decision-making body, then, is the faculty. Students are not a legitimate decision-making body.

LEGITIMACY AND RESPONSIBILITY

The criterion of legitimacy is different in nature from the other two criteria because the legitimacy of faculty educational policy determination is conferred on the faculty. The criteria of competence and responsibility, however, are inherent in the professorial role. The "external" nature of the legitimacy criterion therefore makes it possible for a university to legitimize student decision making on educational matters. While a university can thus legitimize, by fiat or policy, student participation in educational decision making, the criteria of competence and responsibility cannot be satisfied by students.

By definition, students do not have the substantive and experiential competence to make educational decisions. This seems so obvious as not to warrant discussion. Faculty are those who instruct and those who must decide on what to instruct. Students are those who receive instruction and who participate in the instructional process. If students had the professional knowledge, training, and experience of faculty, there would seem to be little point in faculty instructing students. It is therefore difficult to see how students can be considered competent. Students may be intelligent, sensible, and mature. But possession of these qualities does not make them competent in the sense used here.

Responsibility is in some ways the most important of the criteria. It has been said that students should as much as possible be responsible for their own education. We can all agree with this proposition if we clearly specify that we mean student self-education and not the education of other students. The faculty must always think of *all* students, or at least of relatively large segments of students. A student, on the other hand, should think mainly of his own education, even though he may occasionally be interested in the education of other students. The gap between faculty responsibility and stu-

140

dent responsibility is very large. While students have to live with the consequences of decisions that affect them and their education, they are not accountable to anyone.

A decision-making body is always responsible for its decisions. Even if student participation in decision making were legitimized, there is no appropriate way to hold students accountable. Thus we say that students are not responsible—in the educational decision-making sense. They are transient participants in and beneficiaries of the teaching-learning process. As such they cannot be responsible. Professors are officers of instruction. This means that they must work toward the goals of instruction set by themselves and their peers. These goals of instruction are part of educational policy. And the professors themselves, as collective faculty, have the responsibility both for setting the goals and for helping to get to them. Students do not have this responsibility because it is not their function to set educational goals although it is their function to help to get to the goals.

In sum, then, students cannot legitimately participate in the actual educational decision making of the university. They lack the competence to do so, and, perhaps more important, they do not have nor cannot have the responsibility necessary to the decision-making process. If students are to participate in university decision making, then it will be necessary to change the definition of the university, to change its fundamental purposes. Let us now look at some consequences of student participation, but particularly at the effect of such participation on the purposes of the university.

SOME CONSEQUENCES OF STUDENT PARTICIPATION

Before outlining the consequences of student educational decision making, I want to emphasize that I am not advocating student oblivion, isolation, and acquiescence. As I will point out later, students have a legitimate part to play in the whole process of decision making. My main point is the fundamental one of legitimacy, competence, and responsibility in decision making and not one of squelching student interest and involvement in larger university affairs. On the contrary, faculty should be sensitive to student needs and opinions, and appropriate ways and means should be found to involve students in the policy-making process. This process, however, should not include equal rights in debating and voting.

If students participate in university decisions on educational matters to the extent of debating and voting, the consequences will be serious and far-reaching. The university as we know it will be altered radically, and society and the students themselves will suffer because one of the two important functions of the professor, instruction, will be undermined. We must now assume, as we did earlier, that instruction is solely the function of the professor. This means that professors and only professors determine broad educational policy and the implementation of policy in the classroom. That this has been only partially the case in American universities does not alter the validity of the proposition. But how will student participation in decision making affect professors so severely?

First, it is only recently that the professors of many universities have been able to exercise the educational decision-making function that is rightfully theirs. In many institutions faculty decision making has been weak. The real power has been held by administrators. To be sure, in some institutions —the strongest ones—the faculty has held decision-making power. It can be said, however, that faculty decision making will be seriously impaired by student participation, but especially in those institutions where faculty power has been weak, because attention and effort will be distracted from the necessity of faculty policy making.

Attention will be focused on students, and the consequences will be discouragement and apathy of faculty and the subsequent strengthening of administration and university bureaucracy, which will have to make policy in the absence of faculty strength and participation. What I am saying, in effect, is that the ultimate struggle will be between students and administration—after the faculty gives up in discouragement and disillusion. The outcome of this struggle will be that the real university power of educational decision making will be in administrative and bureaucratic hands. While administrators may be competent, the effect of administrative policy making will be academic mediocrity.

FACULTY CENTRALITY

The most important part of a university is its faculty. An excellent university means an excellent faculty. Although an excellent institution must have good administrators and good students, the indispensable ingredient of university greatness is faculty excellence. And a potentially excellent faculty cannot function as a faculty without almost complete instructional decision-making power. An outstanding institutional program requires a considerable degree of discussion, planning, commitment, and decision making of constantly interacting and highly involved sets of faculty members who are responsible for the actual implementation of the program.

The second large and deleterious effect of student participation is student disrespect for administrators, professors, and even the university itself. This disrespect springs in good part from faculty and administrator fear of students in educational decision making. If students are permitted to participate in educational decision making it will be partly due to fear. It is true, of course, that many professors disagree with the position expressed in this paper. Many of them believe that students should participate in decision making, even to the point of voting equally with professors. Some espouse this for so-called democratic reasons. Others think that such participation is itself "educational." Many professors and administrators, how-

142

ever, are probably reacting to student pressure, demonstration, and threat. When demands are met through fear rather than through careful, rational, and objective analysis and decision, the way is paved for more demands and ultimate educational defeat.

Sooner or later administrators and faculty will have to resist demands that seriously and obviously disrupt or damage the educational program or the professors or the students themselves. When policy is decided predominantly through pressure, threat, and fear, in other words, there is no adequate basis for future decisions and actions. Each crisis must be met in an ad hoc fashion. Each demand must be met or staved off cautiously and gingerly. But it is obvious that there has to be some end to the demands.

The effect of acquiescence to unreasonable student demands is, as I said above, student disrespect for the administration, the faculty, and the university. Administrative and faculty positions, whether we like it or not, are positions of responsibility and authority. To acquiesce to unreasonable demands is to relinquish responsibility, to abandon authority, and to lay the foundations for institutional weakness and disorganization—and for student disrespect.

LIMITATIONS ON STUDENT POWER

Students have to act responsibly in matters concerning themselves and their work. By definition, they do not have to act responsibly in institutional matters. The responsibility, as indicated earlier, lies with the faculty and the administration. Similarly, student power is legitimately limited to student matters. To think otherwise and to act on the basis of such thinking is to undermine the values of the institution and the institution itself.

The final large consequence of student participation in educational decision making is the most obvious: weakening of curricula, programs, and courses of study and instruction. As I said earlier, students are not likely to have the experience, knowledge, training, and judgment necessary to build curricula and programs and to decide upon highly complex educational problems. Many professors will agree to this obvious proposition, but they will contend that we should give the student "some say." This is a point of view that has nothing to support it. How can we give students "some say," for example, on whether students should take four or five courses a semester, or whether standards of admission should be raised or lowered, or whether examinations should be given and, if given, what kinds of examination should be used? The complexity of the four- or five-course problem puzzles even faculty. The arguments on standards of admission and the pros and cons of examinations are weighty, involved, and highly difficult matters that require broad experience and much investigation, thought, and discussion for sensible decision.

The answer is clear, simple, and direct: Students should be given no uni-

versity or college decision-making power on educational matters. To yield
at all on this is to support popular trends and educational and social band-
wagons that may be quite legitimate outside the university but not in it. One
of the university's intellectual obligations, for instance, is to study, analyze,
and understand racial prejudice. It is not the university's function to re-
make the society that produced the disease and keeps it going, though it is
its function to influence that society. The university is not a political institution. To make it a political institution will deflect it from its basic goals and
values. The inevitable result will be to undermine the integrity and professional competence of faculty, to create a dispiriting mediocrity, and to damage students and their education.

A FINAL NOTE

Does all this mean that students should have no part in university decision
making? No, it does not. Earlier I indicated some of the areas in which students should decide policy. But they should also have some place in university educational decision making. They should be encouraged, for example,
to study educational policies and practices, to criticize them, and to make
their opinions known. To help students better understand educational
policy and practice, they should be encouraged to have representatives
chosen by themselves present at meetings of faculty decision-making bodies.
At these meetings they should also be encouraged to express their reactions
to and opinions about matters being decided. In a word, they should be
given adequate opportunity to influence faculty decisions. Such influence
is legitimate and healthy. Debating and voting privileges equal to those of
the faculty, however, are not healthy. They lead only to the corrosion of one
of the basic purposes of the university, the transmission of knowledge, and
to the weakening of professors, the principal agents of the instructional
function of the university.

ANNOTATED BIBLIOGRAPHY

SELECTED ANNOTATED BIBLIOGRAPHY

Compiled by
PATRICIA J. STICKNEY

Aceto, Thomas D. "Student Participation in Policy Making and the Use of Direct Action at the Mid-West Committee on Institutional Cooperation Universities." Doctoral dissertation. Syracuse University, 1967.

This is a systematic study of attitudes toward student participation in policy making of the dean of students, student government president, chapter president of AAUP, chapter president of Associated Women Students, the student newspaper editor, and the chapter president of SDS in 11 mid-west universities.

Adams, Bernard S. "Where Have All the Heroes Gone?" Working paper prepared for National Association of Student Personnel Administrators. Minneapolis, March, 1968.

The author, the president of Ripon College, advocates that in the formulation of educational institution policy no areas should come under the sole jurisdiction of students, just as no areas should be excluded from their influence. In handling student proposals, university personnel should grant the same academic freedoms of inquiry and expression held by professors.

Austin, C. Gray. "Student Protests and the Establishment." *The Journal of Higher Education.* Vol. 39 (April, 1968), pp. 223-225.

The author suggests that in order to achieve meaningful participation of students decisive and constructive steps must be taken to convince students that they are heard. The administration should work with students in defining a new and permanent place in policy making, and in this way an effective alternative to demonstrations may be created.

Benovich, Joseph B. *et al. Report of the President's Committee on Student Involvement in the University.* Cleveland, Ohio: Cleveland State University, May 16, 1969. (ERIC ED 035 360)

This report includes the findings and recommendations for an expanded student involvement within the existing governmental structures of Cleveland State University. Also included are the findings of a survey of 66 other universities on student involvement in their institutions with brief explanations for their rethinking and revising their policies about student participation in governance.

Bloustein, Edward J. "The New Student and His Role in American Colleges." *Liberal Education.* Vol. 54 (October, 1968), pp. 345-364.

This paper inquires into the resources for and the nature of the student assertion of a right to share in the governance of the American college and university.

Bowles, W. Donald. "Student Participation in Academic Governance." *Education-al Record.* Vol. 49, No. 3 (Summer, 1968), pp. 257-262.

The author, the dean of the College of Arts and Sciences of the American University, offers practical advice on methods by which students can effectively become involved in the decision-making bodies on their campus and eventually share in shaping the academic program.

Boyd, William B. "College Curriculum Design: The Case for More Student Power." *College Board Review.* Vol. 74 (Winter, 1969-70), pp. 7-10.

The author, president of Central Michigan University, comments on the reasons why students seek more legal student power over curriculum. Two barriers are in their way: first, the present power holders (faculty and administrators) must be persuaded or coerced to share their power; second, because of the necessary relationship between power and competence, students, although intellectually as able, lack experience and training. University power should be shared by students, faculty, and administrators, not just divided among them.

Brewster, Kingman, Jr. *Thoughts on University Government.* New Haven, Conn.: Yale University. 1969.

This booklet contains two papers written by the president of Yale University at the beginning and end of the 1968-69 academic year when participation and responsibility in development of university policy and in decision making was a major issue on many campuses. Included is a proposal on ways in which authority might be made more accountable to the university community (e.g., 1. disclosure of current activities and decisions; 2. right of petition of those affected by decisions, and 3. some regular understood process of evaluating the administration). Administrative accountability is more apt to reduce discontent on campuses than is student representation in decision making. (One paper, "The Politics of Academia," is included in this volume, pp. 87-95).

Brunson, May A. "Student Involvement in University Governance: Sense or Nonsense?" *Journal of the National Association of Women Deans and Counselors.* Vol. 32 (Summer, 1969), pp. 169-175.

The author advocates student participation by refuting some of the traditional arguments against student involvement, such as immaturity, transiency, lack of legal responsibility, and apathy. Paper includes examples of various institutional approaches to student participation.

Butts, Porter. "A Case for 'Joint Power' vs. 'Student Power'." *The Bulletin of the Association of College Unions.* Vol. 366 (December, 1968), p. 811.

The author advocates a partnership of students with faculty and administration rather than a separate student power movement.

Caffrey, John (ed.). *The Future Academic Community: Continuing and Change.* Washington, D.C.: American Council on Education, 1969.

This book contains the proceedings of the 1968 annual meeting of the American Council on Education and includes many articles related to student participation in governance (e.g., see articles by C. Peter Magrath, Allan P. Sindler, Robert D. Clark, Edward Schwartz).

Campus Tensions: Analysis and Recommendations. Report of the Special Committee on Campus Tensions. Washington, D.C.: American Council on Education, April, 1970.

This brief report discusses the range of views about campus tensions and how conflicting points of view might be reconciled. Among the recommendations are (1) the processes of academic governance must be seen as essentially fair by all major groups in the academic community; (2) attempts must be made to establish effective communications (e.g., centralized files, rumor centers, ombudsmen, official campus newspapers); (3) joint administrative-faculty-student committees should be established as an aid to effective decision making; and (4) members of the campus community must be commited to the principle of institutional self-governance and its attendant responsibility.

Cole, Joseph. "Student Involvement in Institutional Government: Roles and Relationships." Working paper prepared for the National Association of Student Personnel Administrators. Minneapolis, March, 1968.

The author, the vice-provost for student affairs of the University of Rochester, analyzes four models of university governance which allow greater or less opportunities for student growth: community government model; parallel government model; scramble government model; denial model. Responsibility, both of students and staff, is the key to preventing uncontrolled behavior and a lack of concern.

Collins, Charles G. "Student Rights and Due Process." *Junior College Journal.* Vol. 37 (April, 1967), p. 34ff.

The author suggests that each part of the academic community should participate in decision making in order to minimize any potential conflicts. Students can best be taught democratic processes by direct participation in them.

———. "Student Rights and Freedoms: Toward Implementation Models." Paper read at American Association of Junior Colleges, Honolulu, March, 1970. (ERIC ED 038 936)

The author, associate director of the Junior College Leadership Program of the University of California at Berkeley, suggests that student power must be achieved by confrontation, by incorporating students into the power structure, or be seeking equilization of power judicially. Several models for inclusion of students in policy making are analyzed.

Constructive Changes to Ease Campus Tensions. Office of Institutional Research, National Association of State Universities and Land-Grant Colleges, 1968. (ERIC ED 035 384)

This report documents extensive changes in governance in 113 state and land-grant institutions, showing responses to demands for student involvement in campus policy and for campus reform. This survey report is divided into two broad areas: (1) student participation in university policy making; and (2) policies and procedures on conduct and disruption. The conclusion of the finding is that sharing power with students in campus governance has been intensified and expanded in recent years, and that universities are taking major steps to eliminate the courses of legitimate student discontent.

Crouch, Colin. "Three Approaches to Student Participation." In *Students Today,* Young Fabian Pamphlet 17. London: Fabian Society, 1968. Pp. 16-21.

The author, as the president of the Student Union of the London School of Economics, speaks for inclusion of student representation in university policy making that will enable students to participate fully in the constructive reform of the universities, while noting that heeding the call by the left or maintaining the status quo are sure to be ineffective.

Cutler, Richard L. "The New Role of the Student in the Academic Society." In *Current Issues in Higher-Education, 1966.* Washington: Association for Higher Education, 1966. Pp. 154-157.

The author, the vice-president for student affairs at the University of Michigan, advocates that universities serve as models by involving students in decision-making processes, thus preparing students to become effective participating citizens in the nation.

Davis, John B., Jr. "A Survey of Practices Related to Student Membership on Academic Committees" A report for the Faculty Senate Committee on Committees. Greenville, N.C.: East Carolina University, 1969.

This study of 49 institutions identifies current campus practices concerning student membership in academic committees and in certain university governing bodies. It is a good assessment of student participation in governance.

Deegan, William L., T.R. McConnell, Kenneth P. Mortimer, and Harriet Stull. *Joint Participation in Decision Making.* Berkeley: Center for Research and Development in Higher Education, University of California, Berkeley, 1970. (ERIC Reading List, ED 038 109)

This study of faculty governance at Fresno State College discusses the composition, functions, operations, and interrelationships of senate and college communities and the general problems of joint participation of faculty and administration in decision making. Although the participation of students in policy making was not studied, there is an examination of ways to fruitful collaboration among all the elements of the college community.

Desmond, Richard. "Faculty and Student Frustrations Shaping the Future of the University." *AAUP Bulletin.* Vol. 55 (March, 1969), pp. 23-26.

The author, the assistant to the vice president and dean of faculties at Illinois State University, calls for the faculty and administration to encourage meaningful student participation in decision making about educational objectives, methods to be used, and the best use of resources and personnel.

Dixon, James P. "Who Will Shape the College?" *Antioch News.* Vol. 44 (April, 1967).

The president of Antioch College discusses that the development of issues concerning how the nature, depth, and extent of change in higher education will be controlled as students increasingly participate in policy making.

Dobbins, Charles G. "The Potentialities of New Things," *Journal of the National Association of Women Deans and Counselors.* Vol. 32 (Summer, 1969), pp. 155-161.

This paper states a case for including students in decision making on the basis that enrich their education and will confirm their membership in the academic community. Educators should be open to students' viewpoints and should assist students in directing their energies to designing better educational programs in a constructive and rehabilitative fashion.

Eddy, Edward D. "Student Involvement in Educational Policy." Paper read at American Council on Education, Washington, D.C., October, 1965.

The author, the president of Chatham College, advocates a greater role for students in shaping educational policy, but he suggests that primary responsibility for educational policy should remain with administrators and faculty.

Enarson, Harold L. "Campus Unrest and Campus Reform." In R.H. Kroepoch, and D.P. Buch (eds.), *Governing the Restless Campus.* Boulder, Colorado: WICHE, (February, 1970). Pp. 3-8.

The president of Cleveland State University analyzes the reasons for student unrest and protest and suggests that academic reform might be accomplished by substituting the learning society for the credentialing society; modernizing the university curriculum; and restructuring and reinvigorating campus governance.

Fellman, David. "Faculty Power vs. Student Power: Collision Course?" *Liberal Education.* Vol. 56 (March, 1970), pp. 61-69.

The paper speaks for trustees, faculty administrators, and students working together, each concentrating on what he can do best and then communicating with one another in every way possible. The author suggests that, in discussions on appointments, promotions, and tenure, although student opinion should be considered, the decisions should be the result of the best professional judgment in the academic community.

150

Fitzgerald, Father Thomas R. *Address*. Presented at 50th Annual Meeting of College and University Business Officers, White Sulphure Springs, November, 1969.

The author, the academic vice-president of Georgetown University, reviews some of the problems in various kinds of changes in university governance. He cites how students want to participate in planning, help formulate institutional goals, help allocate funds and resources, participate in faculty and student recruitment, and assist in curriculum development and in determination of rules of campus life.

Fleming, R.W. "An Administrator's View." *The Illinois State University Journal.* Vol. 32 (December, 1969), pp. 6-21.

The author, the president of the University of Michigan, discusses several models of university governance in which students may find satisfactory roles. There is an analysis of different ways in which changes in university governance can be effected, with a discussion of how many of the functions that students are interested in changing reside at different administrative levels.

Foote, Caleb, Henry Mayer, *et al. The Culture of the University: Governance and Education*. San Francisco: Jossey-Bass Inc., 1968.

This report of the Study Commission on University Governance created at the University of California, Berkeley, in January, 1967, in the wake of violent student disorders, puts forth a series of recommendations on redesigning the system of governance of a university. One recommendation is that effective student participation should be achieved through their involvement on faculty and administrative committees, particularly at the departmental level.

Footlick, Jerrold K. "A Testing by Protest." *The College Scene Now.* Silver Spring, Maryland: Dow Jones, 1967.

The author presents some of the arguments for and against student involvement in decision making. Students generally have more influence at the better educational institutions and are gaining power throughout the country through the use of protest. Students are gaining influence in areas traditionally the responsibility of faculty: curriculum, hiring, promotion, and tenure. For the future, the author predicts a student-faculty confrontation.

Flynn, Magnus. "A Survey of Student Involvement in the Decision Making Process at Canadian Universities." *The Journal of the Canadian Association of University Student Personnel Services.* Vol. 2 (Spring, 1967), pp. 12-14.

This is a report of a survey of 31 Canadian universities regarding student participation in the decision-making process. The author, the dean of students at Sir George Williams University, speaks in favor of greater student roles and responsibilities in university governance.

Frankel, Charles. *Education and the Barricades*. New York: W. W. Norton & Co., 1968.

This book clarifies the basic issues provoking the troubles on American campuses, so that reforms can be designed on sound educational grounds. The precise meaning and limits of the term "student power" are analyzed with respect to particular educational issues—curriculum reform, selection of faculty, and student discipline. The political structure of universities is examined with attention to student rights and the enhancement of student power over the decision-making functions of a university. ("The Structure of Universities" is included in this volume, pp. 112-124.)

Frick, Ivan E. "Reflections on Participatory Democracy." *Liberal Education.* Vol. 55, No. 2 (May, 1969), pp. 262-271.

The author, the president of Findley College, reflects on decision making in colleges and universities, with an understanding of the climate of learning and consideration of the interactions of college constituencies.

Gerth, Donald R. "The Roles of Students in Governance: Student Rights, Privileges, Freedoms and Responsibilities." Report to Academic Senate at the California State Colleges, January 7, 1966.

Golden, M.P. and N. A. Rosen. "Student Attitudes Toward Participation in University Administration: An Empirical Study Related to Managerial Prerogatives." *The Journal of College Student Personnel.* Vol. 7 (November, 1966), pp. 323-330.

This report presents findings of a study on student attitudes toward participation in university administration in three New York colleges.

Gould, Samuel B. "The Role of the Student in the Life of the University." *NASPA,* Vol. 4 (October, 1966), pp. 53-58.

The author, the president of the State University of New York, discusses ways to encourage a campus climate that fosters mature student participation: emphasizing the central role of education in society; providing for more student participation in campus governance; increasing dialogue between students and faculty outside the classroom; encouraging more effective student government; and supporting student involvement in community affairs.

"Governing a College: How Much Should Students Have to Say?" CM Front Line Report, *College Management.* Vol. 4, No. 5 (May, 1969), pp. 30-39.

The views of 212 deans of students were obtained by *College Management* on the amount of student participation in decision making in the following areas: clubs, dorm rules, discipline, curriculum, faculty appointment, admissions, endowment use, and selection of a president.

"Governing a College—The Role Students Play: A Unified Command." *College Management.* Vol. 4, No. 5 (May, 1969), pp. 48-49.

This article discusses how the University of New Hampshire employs a unicameral system that involves students, faculty, graduate students, and administration.

"Governing a College—The Role Students Play: Curriculum, Yes; Social Life, No." *College Management.* Vol. 4, No. 5 (May, 1969), pp. 53-54.

This paper discusses the unusual situation at Guilford College, a Quaker institution where students have a lot to say about curriculum but nothing about dorm rules and social life.

"Governing a College—The Role Students Play: Students Can Help Plan Curriculum Changes," *College Management.* Vol. 4, No. 5 (May, 1969), pp. 50-52.

This paper discusses how Hiram College student and faculty members have been able to prove that teaching and learning and curriculum choices do go together.

"Governing a College—The Role Students Play: The Pros and Cons of Student Involvement." *College Management.* Vol. 4., No. 5 (May, 1969), pp. 40-44.

Two faculty members at the University of Delaware debate the role students should play in the selection and retention of faculty and in curriculum decisions.

"Governing a College—The Role Students Play: Whose Man is the Chancellor?" *College Management.* Vol. 4, No. 5 (May, 1969), pp. 56-60.

This article discusses a case at Syracuse University in which the trustees appointed a chancellor by involving students and faculty in the selection. How this experience in joint decision making has affected changes in this campus governance is also discussed.

"Governing a College—The Role Students Play: Two Heads are Better than One." *College Management.* Vol. 4, No. 5 (May, 1969), pp. 45-47.

The paper discusses the Dickinson College proposal for a bicameral system of institutional governance that will give faculty and students a greater voice but will not involve them directly in every single decision.

Governance: Compendium Series of Current Research, Programs and Proposals 1. Washington, D.C.: ERIC Clearinghouse on Higher Education, (May, 1970).

An annotated compendium describing relevant general and institutional studies concerned with governance. Each item is listed alphabetically by title of project, with anticipated publication dates given for studies now in progress and with source of availability of completed report.

"Governing Boards: Trustees Strive to Close Generation Gap—But Not by Opening Board to Students." *College and University Business* (April, 1969), p. 24.

This brief article gives a flavor on how university trustees want to be in communication with students but resist changes which would include students in decision making on governing boards.

Halladay, D.W. "The Role of The Student." *Leadership and Responsibility on the Changing Campus: Who's in Charge Here?* Papers presented at American Association of State Colleges and Universities. Washington: AASCU, 1969. Pp. 47-49.

The author considers legitimate student demands regarding the quality of educational experience such as: the faculty's disaffection from basic function of good teaching, the relevance of curriculum offerings, and the teaching relationship between teacher and student. In order to insure the quality of education, there should be a program of meaningful student representation in campus policy and planning groups.

Heffner, Ray L. "The Student Voice in Institutional Policy." Association of Governing Boards of Universities and Colleges, *AGB Reports.* Vol. 10, No. 5 (February, 1968), pp. 3-10.

The president of Brown University states that all elements of the academic community need to understand and accept the institutional goals. In the formulation of institutional policy, students can and have been included. Students are accepted as junior partners while preserving the authority of the president and the governing board. Alternatives are provided in which experimental approaches can develop, so that parts of the community, such as students, are not faced with only the choice of accepting or rejecting "the system."

Heyns, Roger W. "The Nature of the Academic Community." Paper read at College Student Personnel Institute, Claremont, California, November, 1966.

The author, chancellor of the University of California, Berkeley, discusses in this paper the purpose and role of the academic community, which, due to lack of clarity in definition has resulted in student unrest and an inordinate amount of time spent on university governance.

Hodgkinson, Harold L. "Campus Governance—The Next Decade." *The Research Reporter.* Vol. 5, No. 1. Berkeley: Center for Research and Development in Higher Education, University of California, 1970. (ERIC ED 039 845)

In this article the author predicts an increasing number of adversary situations in campus governance during the next decade and makes suggestions for the decentralization of decision making.

———. "Governance and Factions—Who Decides Who Decides?" *The Research Reporter* Vol. 3, No. 3. Berkeley: Center for Research and Development in Higher Education, University of California, 1968.

Various problems in campus governance are pointed up and several ways to improve governance are suggested: (1) set up a university-wide governing body composed of representatives of all factions; (2) give administrators more power than they now possess; and (3) make decisions on a nonrepresentative, ad hoc basis by all concerned with a particular issue.

———. "Governance and Factions—Who Decides Who Decides?" *The Research Reporter.* Vol. 3, No. 3, pp. 4-7. Berkeley: Center for Research and Development

153

in Higher Education, University of California, 1968. Also in G. Kerry Smith (ed.), *Agony and Promise: Current Issues in Higher Education.* San Francisco: Jossey-Bass, Inc., 1969. Pp. 139-144.

Preliminary findings of the American Association for Higher Education's Campus Governance Project reveal that governance patterns are difficult to change in part due to tradition, to the self interests of those involved, and to the fact that most institutional change is gradual.

————. "Students and an Intellectual Community." *Educational Record.* Vol. 49, No. 4 (Fall, 1968), pp. 398-406.

The author puts forth that self-interest collaboration, replacing today's faculty-student-administration conflict, will come when the competing elements "see the necessity for collaboration in order to achieve individual goals."

————. "Students and Academic Responsibility." Paper read at American Association for Higher Education Conference. Stillwater, Minn., November, 1967.

The author suggests that students, faculty, and administrators compete instead of work together toward mutual goals; as bargaining power increases, conflict intensifies. Various ways students can participate meaningfully in the operation of colleges are suggested.

————. "Student Participation in Campus Governance." Paper presented at American Educational Research Association. Los Angeles, February, 1969. (ERIC reading list ED 034 478)

The report and analysis of students' role in governance is based upon the findings of a questionnarie administered to 3000 persons on 19 campuses and in more than 900 interviews. A variety of patterns of student involvement, both qualitatively and quantitatively, was found. Three types of responses were: (1) student participation was favored in the belief that better decisions would result: (2) students had been included in decision making to "take the heat off," and (3) administrators believed students should have no say, while the faculty agreed with the administrators and students simultaneously.

————. "Student Protest—An Institutional and National Profile," *Teachers College Record.* May, 1970, pp. 537-555.

This is a report of a study of over 1200 institutions to identify characteristics of those with increased student protest. One finding was that increased student involvement in decision making did not result in a decrease in student protest.

————. and Richard L. Muth, (eds). *Power and Authority: Transformation of Campus Governance.* San Francisco: Jossey-Bass, Inc., 1971.

This collection of thirteen points of view on campus governance provides a source book of analyses and proposals. For example, Kingman Brewster advocates student participation in governance, but only to the extent of holding the administration accountable to the student body as well as to other constituencies. Robert Powell clarifies that student power is fundamentally an educational principle, not a political one, and offers specific suggestions for a democratic university.

Homer, J.T. and R.L. Horner. "Student Involvement in Governance and Administration of Higher Education." *NASPA,* Vol. 4 (October, 1966), pp. 59-64.

This article reviews the history, nature, and extent of the student's role in decision making in universities in the 1950's and 1960's.

"Issues in University Governance." A report to the Ford Foundation on the Summer Colloquium on University Governance. New York: Institute of Higher Education, Department of Higher and Adult Education, Teachers College, Columbia University, September, 1968.

This publication contains summaries of papers presented during a five-week colloquium on university governance. The papers by Franklin Littell, Allan Westin, W. H. Crowley, and Carl Davidson focus on student participation in governance.

Jenks, R. Stephen *et al. Report of the Government Organization.* Durham, New Hampshire University, New Hampshire: March, 1969. (ERIC ED 034 500)

This report by the Committee on Government Organization of the University of New Hampshire presents a unicameral government structure with supporting student and faculty caucuses.

Johnstone, D. Bruce, "The Student and His Power." *The Journal of Higher Education.* Vol. 40 (March, 1969), pp. 205-218.

The author discusses six methods of exercising student power which would bring students into an effective decision-making role: (1) lower-level planning, such as joint planning of individual courses on a departmental level; (2) individual programs, such as independent study and credit by examination; (3) indications of consumer preference; (4) involvement in faculty reward system, such as course and teacher evaluations, and compelling faculty to assist students in preparation for externally administered examinations; (5) exposure to experimental colleges; and (6) the expression of dissent, such as an underground press. The author analyzes the limitations of various traditional mechanisms of student involvement. (This article is also included in this volume, pp. 95-105).

Joughin, Louis. "The Role of the Student in College and University Government." Paper read at the Symposium on Academic Freedom and Responsibility. Los Angeles, California State College, May, 1968. (ERIC reading list ED 034 479)

The author discusses areas and ways for student participation in campus governance.

Kauffman, Joseph F. "The Role of The Student." *Leadership and Responsibility on the Changing Campus: Who's in Charge Here?* Papers presented at the American Association of State Colleges and Universities. Washington: The Association, 1968. Pp. 49-51.

The author advocates a developmental approach toward student involvement in decision making and therefore believes the improvement of human relationships within the educational institution to be of first importance.

Keeton, Morris. *A Productive Voice for Students.* Working Paper prepared for the National Summer Conference for Academic Deans, July 31, 1967. American Association for Higher Education. January, 1968.

The author, the academic vice-president of Antioch College, advocates that productivity in terms of institutional objectives should be the criterion for student participation in university governance. Allocating responsibility to students and evaluating their management of those responsibilities is very important to a liberal education and crucial to a democratic society.

———. *Shared Authority on Campus.* Washington, D.C.: American Association for Higher Education, 1971.

The author analyzes methods of governance in 19 campuses and recommends approaches that could be used to improve the effectiveness of governance by increasing trust and cooperation among the constituent groups.

Kerlinger, Fred N. "Student Participation in University Educational Decision Making." *Teachers College Record.* Vol. 70 (October, 1968), pp. 45-51.

The author argues against giving students decision-making power in colleges and universities. The three criteria on which he bases his stand are legitimacy, responsibility, and competence, and he explains how their application would disqualify students from participation in governance. (Also included in this volume, pp. 138-147.)

Keyes, Ralph. "Student Involvement: The Why and How." *NASPA,* Vol. 6 (October, 1968), pp. 77-82.

The author, graduate student at the London School of Economics, states several reasons why student involvement in academic planning is advisable on purely practical grounds. Some of the problems in defining the student role in campus decision making are noted, with a hope that all campus groups can meet as people, not as power blocks, to work on and solve major educational problems.

Kilcoyne, Francis P. "Some Observations on the Governance of Institutions of Higher Education." Paper read at 50th Annual Meeting of College and University Business Officers. White Sulphur Springs, November, 1969.

The paper discusses the role and responsibilities of faculty, administrators, and trustees. Although consultation with students may be helpful, the author points up some of the problems in student involvement in campus governance.

Knorr, Owen A. and John W. Minter (eds.) *Order and Freedom on the Campus: The Rights and Responsibilities of Faculty and Students.* Boulder, Colorado: Western Interstate Commission for Higher Education, 1965. (ERIC ED 032 856)

These papers and discussions of the Seventh Annual Institute for College and University Self Study in Berkeley, sponsored by WICHE and the Center for Higher Education, deal with the nature of student-faculty-administration relationships and the resulting discontent and tension on college and university campuses.

Levi, Julian H. "Student Unrest and the Role of Student Participation in Institutional Government." *The College Counsel.* Vol. 4, No. 2 (1969) pp. 23-43.

Lipscomb, Greg. "Some Concepts of Student Academic Freedom." Paper read at the American Council on Education. Washington, D.C., October, 1965.

The author, who at the time was a student at the University of Texas, advocates a greater role for students in the total academic community, including a functional part in defining academic freedom, developing academic standards, determining administration procedures, and making decisions on any other process that affects students.

Locklin, R.H. and C.T. Stewart. "Student, Faculty and Administrator Perceptions of Decision-Making at Four Colleges." Paper read at American Educational Research Association. Minneapolis, March, 1970.

This is a report on a study of four colleges regarding student and faculty attitudes around policy making in 38 different areas. In general, results showed that students desire more power than faculty-administrators want to give them; intergroup relations are colored by each group's misconceptions of the other group's desire; and dominant unitary norms related to individual behavior do not exist either among students or faculty-administrators.

Long, Durward. "The Impact of Activist Students in Changing the Governance and Culture of the Campus." Paper read at 25th National Conference on Higher Education. Chicago, March, 1970. (ERIC ED 039 852)

The author, vice chancellor of the University of Wisconsin Center System, reports on how the efforts of student activists have brought a recognition of the need for reform in higher education and the introduction of new student culture. As a result, new governance and procedure models dealing with academic issues as well as those issues affecting student life are being developed with students.

Lunn, Harry H., Jr. *The Student's Role in College Policy Making.* A Report prepared for the Commission on Student Personnel. Washington, D.C.: American Council on Education, 1957.

This report for the Commission on Student Personnel describes different forms of student involvement in administration and policy formulation.

Macneil, Ian. "The President's Commission on Student Involvement in Decision-Making: A Comment," Ithaca, N.Y.: Cornell University, 1969. Mimeographed. (ERIC Reading List ED 034 502).

This comment directed to individuals at Cornell University focuses on relationships between student involvement in making and intellectual liberty. It recommends that before any significant change in the university can take place, the impact of such change on academic freedom should be thought through and carefully considered.

Mann, Carl, "Academic Governance on an Urban Campus: Role Expectations of Faculty and Students." Doctoral dissertation. Columbia University Teachers College, 1969.

This dissertation analyzes the student and faculty role expectations in institutional decision making in such areas as: academic matters, campus facilities, professional personnel, financial affairs, campus conduct, student organizations, and public relations.

Marchese, Theodore J. "Student Participation in Plans Is No Longer A Question of Whether, But How?" *College and University Business*. Vol. 47, (August, 1969), pp. 37-38.

The author argues for genuinely involving students in governance, because it would be a means to improve the range and quality of advice while enlarging and enriching the input into the planning process. Also, student participation would provide maximum opportunity for student development and fulfillment.

Martin, Warren Bryan. "Student Participation in Academic Governance." *Current Issues in Higher Education, 1967: In Search of Leaders*. Washington, D.C.: American Association for Higher Education, 1967. Pp. 173-77.

The author advocates greater student involvement in academic policy formation and institutional governance, and lists and then refutes the usual arguments against such participation. He proposes a university-wide council in which faculty, students, and administrators would share in the development and implementation of policy.

McConnell, T.R. *The Redistribution of Power in Higher Education: Changing Patterns of Internal Governance*. Berkeley: Center for Research and Development in Higher Education, University of California at Berkeley, 1971.

This is a discussion of governance within higher educational institutions and the changes that have been and must be made as institutions are forced to deal with new situations and non-traditional values.

McDonough, John R. "The Role of Students in Governing the University." *AGB Reports*. Vol. 10, No. 7 (April, 1968), pp. 24-31.

From his experience on the Committee of 15 established at Stanford University to discuss university problems and policies, the author advocates that students should be heard on matters of legitimate interest to them, by means of advising, assisting, and advocating rather than deciding.

McGehee, Nan E. "Faculty and Students, or Faculty Versus Students." Washington, D.C.: National Association of State Universities and Land Grant Colleges, 1969. Mimeographed. (ERIC Reading List)

This paper analyzes the four most common issues students raise in their demand for participation in the decision-making processes of the university. The author suggests that conflicts arise from the differing perceptions of university goals.

McGrath, Earl J. *Should Students Share the Power? A Study of Their Role in College and University Governance*. Philadelphia, Pa.: Temple University Press, 1970.

The author, a former U.S. Commissioner of Education and former director of higher education centers at Columbia and at Temple, undertook for the American Academy of Arts and Sciences the study of the student's stake in university governance. This excellent and factual book includes a report on existing practices in over 900 institutions, opinions on their effectiveness, recommendations concerning desirable policies as experience and reason seem to support, and an extensive bibliography of pertinent literature on student participation. "For and Against Student Participation" is also included in this volume, pp. 124-133.

Milton, Ohmer. *Survey of Faculty Views on Student Participation in Decision Making.* Final Report, No. 7-D-037. Washington, D.C.: U.S. Office of Education, Department of Health, Education, and Welfare. Bureau of Research, Final Report Project, May, 1968.

A selected group of full-time faculty and administrators in six schools were interviewed to ascertain their attitudes or opinions about student involvement in determining cogent campus policies regarding decision making in the following eight areas: student discipline, evaluation of teachers, academic calendar arrangements, curriculum planning, degree requirements, grading systems, faculty governing boards, and legal governing boards.

Mitau, G. Theodore. "Student Participation in Campus Government." Paper read at Student Convention. St. Cloud State College, St. Cloud, Minnesota, February, 1969. (ERIC Reading List ED 029 563)

The author believes that participatory campus democracy is necessary if colleges and universities want to continue to be viable and dynamic. He proposes that students be involved in all university decisions that affect their personal lives, curricula, and campus environment.

Morris, Arval A. "Student Participation in University Decision Making." Mimeographed, 1969. (ERIC Reading List)

In analyzing the causes of student rebellion against established social and educational systems, the author suggests various areas for and the use of the principle of consultation and accommodation as a guide to solving the problem of student participation in university decision making. This article generally opposes extending student participation in decision making.

Morison, Robert S. *Students and Decision Making.* Washington, D.C.: Public Affairs Press, 1970.

This is the chairman's report of Cornell University's Commission on Student Involvement in Decision Making. It advocates greater student participation in university governance.

Mundinger, Donald C. "Due Process and the College Student." Paper read at American Council on Education. Washington, D.C., October, 1965.

This paper stresses the growing importance of due process on campuses, particularly as students seek greater participation in social and academic decision making.

Murphy, Franklin D. Address. Presented at American Council on Education. Denver, October, 1968.

This paper comments on the role and responsibilities of university board of trustees and its chairman and president. Students, more concerned with today than tomorrow, should be included in discussions where short-term policies are being formulated.

Muston, Ray A. "Governance Changes are Catching Colleges by Surprise, National Survey Shows." *College and University Business,* Vol. 47, (July, 1969), pp. 29-31.

Researchers at Indiana University report on a survey conducted in 1968 of 1769 institutions of higher education about their policy boards, and on a follow-up survey in 1969 concerning significant changes in governance.

NASPA Ad Hoc Committee on Student Power. "Special: Statement on Student Power." *NASPA*. Vol. 6 (October, 1968), pp. 87-89.

The National Association of Student Personnel Administrators (NASPA) Statement on Student Power analyzes the conditions that contribute to legitimate student power: general acceptance of the legitimacy of disagreement, emergence of students who have an understanding of educational issues and employ constructive methods; administrative acceptance of these students as participants in decision making; and the introduction of innovative learning and teaching procedures. The Statement also includes analysis of forces that work against student power. Although constructive use of student power cannot be based on a one-man, one-vote concept, it is predicated on the worth of ideas.

Neff, Charles B. "The Administrative Challenge of the New Student Activism." *The Journal of Higher Education*. Vol. 39 (February, 1968), pp. 69-76.

The paper discusses the reasons why administrators should encourage student participation in overall curriculum planning, particularly where discussion of course content, teaching, and research is most useful and where students have most competence. As students have not been meaningfully involved in campus governance and are rebelling against flows in higher education, student activists frequently attack campus administration from the outside, focusing on regulatory policy rather than on educational policy.

Otten, C. Michael. *University Authority and the Student: The Berkeley Experience*. Berkeley, California: University of California Press, 1970.

The author uses the University of California, especially at Berkeley, as a historical case study in analyzing the present crisis on American campuses in terms of inherent dilemmas of organizational control, and contends that the crises are not the ones of specific political issues but arise from the demand for democratization of organizational power, both within and outside the university.

Peterson, Martha E. "Student Activities: A 1969 Appraisal." *Journal of the National Association of Women Deans and Counselors*. Vol. 32 (Summer, 1969), pp. 188-190.

The author, the president of Barnard College, appraises the student demands in 1969 and realizes that academic communities which have made students peripheral must now undergo major changes, even upheaval, as students take their place as active members.

Powell, Lewis F., Jr. "Critical Issues and Leadership on Today's Campus." *Leadership and Responsibility on the Changing Campus: Who's in Charge Here?* Papers presented at American Association of State Colleges and Universities. Washington, D.C.: The Association, 1968. Pp. 1-7.

The author advocates that students should have a voice, but not to the degree that students in Latin American universities have.

Powell, Robert S., Jr. "Student Power and the Student Role in Institutional Governance." *Liberal Education*. Vol. 55 (March, 1969), pp. 24-31.

The paper discusses the student desire to share the responsibility of decision making and the student role in institutional governance.

Proposed Alterations in the Governance of the University. Stanford Chapter, American Association of University Professors, 1968. (ERIC ED 035 355)

A series of recommendations for Stanford University are made: a request for a greater quantity of timely information relevant to major decisions, and an urging for increased faculty and student participation in the decision-making process. The trustees and president, who have final authority, should make decisions only after consultation and with full opportunity for expression of dissenting views.

Robinson, Lora H. and Janet D. Shoenfeld. *Student Participation in Academic Governance.* Review No. 1. Washington, D.C.: ERIC Clearinghouse on Higher Education, The George Washington University, February, 1970. (ERIC Reading List ED 035 786)

This booklet on student participation includes a review of trends and findings in the literature documenting the nature and extent of student participation, and annotated bibliography, and a compendium of recent institutional changes in colleges and universities which have increased student participation in governance. The six main sections are: surveys of general practices; surveys of attitudes; arguements for, against, and about student participation; hypothetical models of governance, methods of increasing student involvement; and institutional proposals to increase student involvement or establish new governance structures.

Sanford, Nevitt. "A Professor's View." *The Illinois State University Journal.* Vol. 32 (December, 1969), pp. 22-38.

A professor at Stanford University discusses his views on ways to give students experience in relevant decision making in a democracy.

Schoen, Walter Thomas, Jr. "Clarification and Delineation of Areas of Student and Faculty Responsibility." *The Journal of College Student Personnel.* Vol. 6 (June, 1965), pp. 244-246.

The article speaks for a clear definition of the distinct and joint areas of student, faculty, and administration responsibilities.

Schwab, Joseph J. *College Curriculum and Student Protest.* Chicago: University of Chicago Press, 1969.

This book, written by a University of Chicago professor, explores the college and university curriculum in light of student activism and student demand for a share in decision making.

Schwartz, Edward (ed.). *Student Power: A Collection of Readings.* Washington, D.C.: U.S. National Student Association, January, 1969.

This anthology has three purposes: (1) to make available essays by students on the definition and meaning of student power; (2) to highlight specific proposals for including students into the campus decision-making process; and (3) to examine in detail several campus confrontations in order to provide some collective wisdom from these experiences.

Schwartz, Edward. "Student Power—In Response to the Questions." In John Caffrey (ed.) *The Future Academic Community: Continuity and Change.* Washington: American Council on Education, 1969. Pp. 56-67.

The author analyzes why students want more say about parietal rules, the curriculum, the quality of teaching, and university priorities. The student power movement appears to be more concerned with the "kind of rule" and "the qualities of human rules" than with "who rules."

Schwebel, Robert. "Wakening Our Sleepy Universities: Student Involvement in Curriculum Change." *Teachers College Record.* Vol. 70 (October, 1968), pp. 31-43.

The author, then a student at Antioch College, gives specific examples of student involvement in effecting curriculum changes from both within and outside the existing university structures.

Shaffer, Jay C. "Students in the Policy Process." *The Journal of Higher Education.* Vol. 41, No. 5 (1970), pp. 341-349.

The author, a former head of student government at Ohio State University, advocates formal integration of students into the university policy process and suggests ways the university must attempt to remedy the problems students have in becoming full and effective participants in the policy process. (Also included in this volume, pp. 105-112.)

Shoben, Edward Joseph, Jr. "Student and University Governance: A Preliminary Sketch." Buffalo: State University of New York, 1969. Mimeographed. (ERIC Reading List)

The Head of the Center for Higher Education, State University of New York at Buffalo, states that new university governance structures must allow for personalized forms of representation and must be linked to human goals if one assumes that (1) extensive and effective participation of students in governances is likely to be a permanent feature of academia; (2) student participation legitimately represents their concerns and provides a channel for their contributions; (3) construction of suitable machinery for greater participation is the only process by which students can become fully committed members of the academic community.

Shulman, Carol. *Governance*. Number 1. Washington, D.C.: ERIC Clearinghouse on Higher Education, The George Washington University, 1970. (ERIC Reading List ED 040 308)

This compendium was undertaken to familiarize both old and new investigators with recently completed and ongoing studies in governance, publications, reports, and recommendations. Although primarily devoted to problems of governing a university, this annotated list does describe many projects which study governance from the student point of view.

Skutt, Richard. "The Role of the Student." In *Leadership and Responsibility on the Changing Campus: Who's in Charge Here?* Papers presented at American Association of State Colleges and Universities. Washington, D.C.: The Association, 1968. Pp. 54-57.

The author proposes three ways in which the student's role in the university might develop: acquisition of self-governance, recognition by faculty and administrators of the student's right to be involved in matters affecting his life, and establishment of a true community of scholars.

Slater, Carl, M.D. "Student Participation in Curriculum Planning and Evaluation." *Journal of Medical Education.* Vol. 44 (August, 1969), pp. 675-678.

The author advocates that students should be formal participants in decision making related to curriculum planning in all medical schools. The medical school is an organization that needs ongoing innovation and renewal and requires curriculum planning involving the contributions of many groups, including students. The article includes findings of a survey on the extent and success of student involvement in curriculum planning in American medical schools. (Also included in this volume, pp. 133-138.)

Smith, G. Kerry, ed. *Current Issues in Higher Education. In Search of Leaders.* Washington, D.C.: American Association for Higher Education, 1967. Part 5, "Student Potential," pp. 173-197.

The collection of papers presented at the 22nd National Conference on Higher Education in 1967 focuses on the search for leadership in all areas of American life. Part 5, "Student Potential," includes articles by Warren B. Martin, Edward J. Shoben, Jr., Philip R. Werdell, E.G. Williamson, Roland Liebert, and Edward D. Eddy, on such topics as student participation in decision making, in faculty evaluation, and in student-initiated courses.

Spolyar, Ludwig, J. "Student Power: Threat or Challenge for Student Personnel?" *NASPA.* Vol. 6 (October, 1968), pp. 74-77.

The National Student Association (NSA) student power resolution of 1967 is discussed. The role of student personnel workers in collaborating with students in examining student power movement assumptions is suggested in order to gain for students a more significant role in university affairs.

Straw, Jack. "Participation in Practice." In *Students Today,* Young Fabian Pamphlet 17. London: Fabian Society, 1968. Pp. 22-26.

This paper discusses the inadequacy of student participation in university governance and recommends the establishment of a system of accountability in which all interests in the university community would be represented and in which all those who made decisions would be held accountable for these decisions to the university community.

"Student Power Revisited: A Revision of the June 1968 Statement on Student Power Prepared by the Ad Hoc Committee on Student Power." *NASPA,* January, 1970, p. 127.

The paper analyzes how, as students participate more in decision and policy making, the emphasis for student power movement shifts from procedural and structural issues to improving the quality of learning.

Sturner, William F. "University Governance through the Bicameral Legislature," *The Journal of Higher Education,* Vol. 42, No. 3 (March, 1971), pp. 219-228.

The author advocates a more realistic and equitable distribution of power in higher education through the bicameral legislature, with one house composed of student representatives and the other consisting of faculty and administrators.

Susman, Warren I. "Is Increased Participation in Decision Making Enough?" Paper presented at 25th National Conference of the American Association for Higher Education. Washington, D.C.: American Association for Higher Education, 1970. (ERIC ED 039 847)

The author, a professor of history at Rutgers University, states that although increased student participation in decision making has met with some success, other reforms in governance are needed to make institutions responsive to current needs. He proposes that students be freed to develop new ways in their own self-governance and that universities be forced to reexamine their welfare state functions and to consider the needs of the whole community.

"The Culture of the University: Governance and Education." Berkeley: Report of the Study Commission on University Governance, University of California, Berkeley, January 15, 1968.

This report presents its recommendations for measures to increase student participation in the formulation of university policies, ways to strengthen student government, means of providing due process in disciplinary procedures, and, in general, definition of areas which should be delegated wholly to students or wholly to faculty or administrators.

The Temple Plan for University Governance. Report by Commission on Student Participation in the Policy-Making Process of the University. Philadelphia: Temple University, September, 1968.

The report of the Commission on Student Participation in Policy-Making at Temple University proposes a specific plan and new structures for university governance based on the conclusion that students should participate in a given area of responsibility to the degree that they are especially concerned with that responsibility.

Vaccaro, Louis C. "Power and Conflict in the University: A Search for Solutions." *College and University.* Vol. 44 (Fall, 1968), pp. 97-107.

This analysis and discussion of university power and conflict is based upon the belief that all segments of the academic community should and are capable of contributing positively in the decision-making process of the university.

Werdell, Philip P. "What the Hell Good are Students Anyway?" Paper read at American Association of Junior Colleges. Boston, February, 1968.

The paper states the case for student participation in policy making and presents various models and procedures for greater student involvement in higher education.

Who's in Charge? A Special Report. Baltimore, Maryland: Editorial Projects for Education, 1969. (ERIC Reading List ED 035 357)

This report, prepared by a group associated with the American Alumni Council, analyzes the answer to "Who's in charge here" in American colleges and universities from the points of view of trustees, president, faculty, students, and the public. The roles and problems of college trustees, presidents, faculty, and students in governing their institutions are outlined.

Williamson, E.G. and John L. Cowan. "Student and Academic Freedom." Paper read at National Association of Student Personnel Administrators. Washington, D.C., April, 1965.

The Dean of Students of the University of Minnesota reports on a survey of students, faculty, and administrators at over 850 colleges and universities, regarding their perceptions of student freedoms. Students participate in varying degrees in policy making. Mutual sharing in defining of freedoms is an important liberty to be established.

Wilson, Logan. "Changing University Governance." *Educational Record.* Vol. 50 (Fall, 1969), pp. 388-404.

The president of the American Council on Education analyzes the changing nature of university governance as the tool to facilitate the main business of any academic community education. Students, faculty, and others should participate in decision making if they also accept the responsibility of their increased authority. The right to determine policy should depend on competence, knowledgeability, and willingness to accept responsibility.

Wise, W. Max. "Reflections on New Configurations in Campus Governance." Paper read at the 25th National Conference of the American Association for Higher Education. Washington, D.C.: American Association for Higher Education, 1970.

The author, a professor of higher education at Columbia University Teachers College, analyzes the recent changes in college government and notes that although students and faculty participation has been extensively explored, the roles of administration and trustees have been ignored. Suggestions are made for strengthening the board of trustees and president roles and responsibilities.

Wofford, Harris. "New and Old Actors in Institutional Decision Making." *Current Campus Issues.* Cambridge, Mass: University Consultants, Inc., 1969.

An account of the creation and development of the State University of New York at Old Westbury by its founding president is presented as an experimental institution with students as full partners in the academic world.

Woodring, Paul. *Higher Education for the '70's.* Paper read at American Association of State Colleges and Universities. Atlanta, November, 1969.

The author notes student demands for a role in policy making on all levels of the campus. He believes students can play a useful role in evaluating teaching and determining certain curriculum patterns. Effective participation is possible in institutions small enough that student policy makers can reflect the majority rule.

APPENDIXES

CSWE STATEMENT ON STUDENT PARTICIPATION IN GOVERNANCE OF SCHOOLS OF SOCIAL WORK

CSWE's Committee on Students recognizing that student participation in governance of schools of social work may make a significant contribution to the processes of policy and decision-making within the school, saw the need for a position statement.

The following position statement developed by the Committee on Students and the Commission on Educational Services was approved by CSWE's Board of Directors at its November, 1970 meeting.

"1. Students should participate in the development and determination of appropriate policies and procedures in the school.

2. The selection or appointment of students on appropriate bodies (i.e., where students represent students officially) of the school should be decided by students through whatever process is used by that body to arrive at decisions affecting its constituency.

3. When functioning as a member of a given body of a school, students should have the same rights as any other member of the body. Schools are urged to maximize the potential for student participation by offering encouragement and appropriate support.

4. The number of students on a committee or policy-making or operational body is a significant factor in determining the full and meaningful participation of students and, therefore, should be determined in relation to the purposes and interest of the group.

5. All policies and procedures pertaining to student participation should be communicated annually in written form to students and faculty, and other participants in the educational process."

Reprinted from Social Work Education Reporter, *Vol. 19, No. 1 (December-January, 1971), p. 2.*

STATEMENT ON GOVERNMENT OF COLLEGES AND UNIVERSITIES

AMERICAN ASSOCIATION OF UNIVERSITY PROFESSORS
AMERICAN COUNCIL ON EDUCATION
ASSOCIATION OF GOVERNING BOARDS OF UNIVERSITIES AND COLLEGES

Editorial Note. The Statement which follows is directed to governing board members, administrators, faculty members, students, and other persons in the belief that the colleges and universities of the United States have reached a stage calling for appropriately shared responsibility and cooperative action among the components of the academic institution. The Statement is intended to foster constructive joint thought and action, both within the institutional structure and in protection of its integrity against improper intrusions.

It is not intended that the Statement serve as a blue print for government on a specific campus or as a manual for the regulation of controversy among the components of an academic institution, although it is to be hoped that the principles asserted will lead to the correction of existing weaknesses and assist in the establishment of sound structure and procedures. The Statement does not attempt to cover relations with those outside agencies which increasingly are controlling the resources and influencing the patterns of education in our institutions of higher learning; e.g., the United States Government, the state legislatures, state commissions, interstate associations, or compacts and other interinstitutional arrangements. However, it is hoped that the Statement will be helpful to these agencies in their consideration of educational matters.

Students are referred to in this Statement as an institutional component coordinate in importance with trustees, administrators, and faculty. There is, however, no main section on students. The omission has two causes: (1) the changes now occurring in the status of American students have plainly outdistanced the analysis by the educational community, and an attempt to define the situation without thorough study might prove unfair to student interests, and (2) students do not in fact presently have a significant voice in the government of colleges and universities; it would be unseemly to obscure, by superficial equality of length of statement, what may be a serious lag entitled to separate and full confrontation. The concern for student status felt by the organizations issuing this Statement is embodied in a note "On Student Status" intended to stimulate the educational community to turn its attention to an important need.

Reprinted from Policy Documents and Reports of the AAUP *September, 1969, pp. 26-30, with permission of the American Association of University Professors.*

This Statement, in preparation since 1964, is jointly formulated by the American Association of University Professors, the American Council on Education, and the Association of Governing Boards of Universities and Colleges. On October 12, 1966, the Board of Directors of the ACE took action by which the Council "recognizes the Statement as a significant step forward in the clarification of the respective roles of governing boards, faculties, and administrations," and "commends it to the institutions which are members of the Council." On October 29, 1966, the Council of the AAUP approved the Statement, recommended approval by the Fifty-Third Annual Meeting in April, 1967,[1] and recognized that "continuing joint effort is desirable, in view of the areas left open in the jointly formulated Statement, and the dynamic changes occurring in higher education." On November 18, 1966, the Executive Committee of the AGB took action by which that organization also "recognizes the Statement as a significant step forward in the clarification of the respective roles of governing boards, faculties and administrations," and "commends it to the governing boards which are members of the Association."

I. INTRODUCTION

This Statement is a call to mutual understanding regarding the government of colleges and universities. Understanding, based on community of interest, and producing joint effort, is essential for at least three reasons. First, the academic institution, public or private, often has become less autonomous; buildings, research, and student tuition are supported by funds over which the college or university exercises a diminishing control. Legislative and executive governmental authority, at all levels, plays a part in the making of important decisions in academic policy. If these voices and forces are to be successfully heard and integrated, the academic institution must be in a position to meet them with its own generally unified view. Second, regard for the welfare of the institution remains important despite the mobility and interchange of scholars. Third, a college or university in which all the components are aware of their interdependence, of the usefulness of communication among themselves, and of the force of joint action will enjoy increased capacity to solve educational problems.

II. THE ACADEMIC INSTITUTION: JOINT EFFORT

A. Preliminary Considerations

The variety and complexity of the tasks performed by institutions of higher education produce an inescapable interdependence among governing board, administration, faculty, students, and others. The relationship calls for adequate communication among these components, and full opportunity for appropriate joint planning and effort.

Joint effort in an academic institution will take a variety of forms appropriate to the kinds of situations encountered. In some instances, an initial exploration or recommendation will be made by the president with consideration by the faculty at a later stage; in other instances, a first and essentially definitive recommendation will be made by the faculty, subject

---

[1] The Annual Meeting approved the Statement.

169

to the endorsement of the president and the governing board. In still others, a substantive contribution can be made when student leaders are responsibly involved in the process. Although the variety of such approaches may be wide, at least two general conclusions regarding joint effort seem clearly warranted: (1) important areas of action involve at one time or another the initiating capacity and decision-making participation of all the institutional components, and (2) differences in the weight of each voice, from one point to the next, should be determined by reference to the responsibility of each component for the particular matter at hand, as developed hereinafter.

B. Determination of General Educational Policy

The general educational policy, i.e., the objectives of an institution and the nature, range, and pace of its efforts, is shaped by the institutional charter or by law, by tradition and historical development, by the present needs of the community of the institution, and by the professional aspirations and standards of those directly involved in its work. Every board will wish to go beyond its formal trustee obligation to conserve the accomplishment of the past and to engage seriously with the future; every faculty will seek to conduct an operation worthy of scholarly standards of learning; every administrative officer will strive to meet his charge and to attain the goals of the institution. The interests of all are coordinate and related, and unilateral effort can lead to confusion or conflict. Essential to a solution is a reasonably explicit statement on general educational policy. Operating responsibility and authority, and procedures for continuing review, should be clearly defined in official regulations.

When an educational goal has been established, it becomes the responsibility primarily of the faculty to determine appropriate curriculum and procedures of student instruction.

Special considerations may require particular accommodations: (1) a publicly supported institution may be regulated by statutory provisions, and (2) a church-controlled institution may be limited by its charter or bylaws. When such external requirements influence course content and manner of instruction or research, they impair the educational effectiveness of the institution.

Such matters as major changes in the size or composition of the student body and the relative emphasis to be given to the various elements of the educational and research program should involve participation of governing board, administration, and faculty prior to final decision.

C. Internal Operations of the Institution

The framing and execution of long-range plans, one of the most important aspects of institutional responsibility, should be a central and continuing concern in the academic community.

170

Effective planning demands that the broadest possible exchange of information and opinion should be the rule for communication among the components of a college or university. The channels of communication should be established and maintained by joint endeavor. Distinction should be observed between the institutional system of communication and the system of responsibility for the making of decisions.

A second area calling for joint effort in internal operations is that of decisions regarding existing or prospective physical resources. The board, president, and faculty should all seek agreement on basic decisions regarding buildings and other facilities to be used in the educational work of the institution.

A third area is budgeting. The allocation of resources among competing demands is central in the formal responsibility of the governing board, in the administrative authority of the president, and in the educational function of the faculty. Each component should therefore have a voice in the determination of short and long-range priorities, and each should receive appropriate analyses of past budgetary experience, reports on current budgets and expenditures, and short and long-range budgetary projections. The function of each component in budgetary matters should be understood by all; the allocation of authority will determine the flow of information and the scope of participation in decisions.

Joint effort of a most critical kind must be taken when an institution chooses a new president. The selection of a chief administrative officer should follow upon cooperative search by the governing board and the faculty, taking into consideration the opinions of others who are appropriately interested. The president should be equally qualified to serve both as the executive officer of the governing board and as the chief academic officer of the institution and the faculty. His dual role requires that he be able to interpret to board and faculty the educational views and concepts of institutional government of the other. He should have the confidence of the board and the faculty.

The selection of academic deans and other chief academic officers should be the responsibility of the president with the advice of and in consultation with the appropriate faculty.

Determinations of faculty status, normally based on the recommendations of the faculty groups involved, are discussed in Part V of this Statement; but it should here be noted that the building of a strong faculty requires careful joint effort in such actions as staff selection and promotion and the granting of tenure. Joint action should also govern dismissals; the applicable principles and procedures in these matters are well established.[2]

---

[2]See the 1940 *Statement of Principles on Academic Freedom and Tenure* and the 1958 *Statement on Procedural Standards in Faculty Dismissal Proceedings.* These statements have been jointly approved or adopted by the Association of American Colleges and the American Association of University Professors; the 1940 Statement has been endorsed by numerous learned and scientific societies and educational associations.

D. External Relations of the Institution

Anyone—a member of the governing board, the president or other member of the administration, a member of the faculty, or a member of the student body or the alumni—affects the institution when he speaks of it in public. An individual who speaks unofficially should so indicate. An official spokesman for the institution, the board, the administration, the faculty, or the student body should be guided by established policy.

It should be noted that only the board speaks legally for the whole institution, although it may delegate responsibility to an agent.

The right of a board member, an administrative officer, a faculty member, or a student to speak on general educational questions or about the administration and operations of his own institution is a part of his right as a citizen and should not be abridged by the institution.[3] There exist, of course, legal bounds relating to defamation of character, and there are questions of propriety.

III. THE ACADEMIC INSTITUTION: THE GOVERNING BOARD

The governing board has a special obligation to assure that the history of the college or university shall serve as a prelude and inspiration to the future. The board helps relate the institution to its chief community: e.g., the community college to serve the educational needs of a defined population area or group, the church-controlled college to be cognizant of the announced position of its denomination, and the comprehensive university to discharge the many duties and to accept the appropriate new challenges which are its concern at the several levels of higher education.

The governing board of an institution of higher education in the United States operates, with few exceptions, as the final institutional authority. Private institutions are established by charters; public institutions are established by constitutional or statutory provisions. In private institutions the board is frequently self-perpetuating; in public colleges and universities the present membership of a board may be asked to suggest candidates for appointment. As a whole and individually when the governing board confronts the problem of succession, serious attention should be given to obtaining properly qualified persons. Where public law calls for election of governing board members, means should be found to insure the nomination

---

[3]With respect to faculty members, the 1940 *Statement of Principles on Academic Freedom and Tenure* reads: "The college or university teacher is a citizen, a member of a learned profession, and an officer of an educational institution. When he speaks or writes as a citizen, he should be free from institutional censorship or discipline, but his special position in the community imposes special obligations. As a man of learning and an educational officer, he should remember that the public may judge his profession and his institution by his utterances. Hence he should at all times be accurate, should exercise appropriate restraint, should show respect for the opinion of others, and should make every effort to indicate that he is not an institutional spokesman."

172

of fully suited persons, and the electorate should be informed of the relevant criteria for board membership.

Since the membership of the board may embrace both individual and collective competence of recognized weight, its advice or help may be sought through established channels by other components of the academic community. The governing board of an institution of higher education, while maintaining a general overview, entrusts the conduct of administration to the administrative officers, the president and the deans, and the conduct of teaching and research to the faculty. The board should undertake appropriate self-limitation.

One of the governing board's important tasks is to ensure the publication of codified statements that define the over-all policies and procedures of the institution under its jurisdiction.

The board plays a central role in relating the likely needs of the future to predictable resources; it has the responsibility for husbanding the endowment; it is responsible for obtaining needed capital and operating funds; and in the broadest sense of the term it should pay attention to personnel policy. In order to fulfill these duties, the board should be aided by, and may insist upon, the development of long-range planning by the administration and faculty.

When ignorance or ill-will threatens the institution or any part of it, the governing board must be available for support. In grave crises it will be expected to serve as a champion. Although the action to be taken by it will usually be on behalf of the president, the faculty, or the student body, the board should make clear that the protection it offers to an individual or a group is, in fact, a fundamental defense of the vested interests of society in the educational institution.

IV. THE ACADEMIC INSTITUTION: THE PRESIDENT

The president, as the chief executive officer of an institution of higher education, is measured largely by his capacity for institutional leadership. He shares responsibility for the definition and attainment of goals, for administrative action, and for operating the communications system which links the components of the academic community. He represents his institution to its many publics. His leadership role is supported by delegated authority from the board and faculty.

As the chief planning officer of an institution, the president has a special obligation to innovate and initiate. The degree to which a president can envision new horizons for his institution, and can persuade others to see them and to work toward them, will often constitute the chief measure of his administration.

The president must at times, with or without support, infuse new life into a department; relatedly, he may at times be required, working within the

173

concept of tenure, to solve problems of obsolescence. The president will necessarily utilize the judgments of the faculty, but in the interest of academic standards he may also seek outside evaluations by scholars of acknowledged competence.

It is the duty of the president to see to it that the standards and procedures in operational use within the college or university conform to the policy established by the governing board and to the standards of sound academic practice. It is also incumbent on the president to insure that faculty views, including dissenting views, are presented to the board in those areas and on those issues where responsibilities are shared. Similarly the faculty should be informed of the views of the board and the administration on like issues.

The president is largely responsible for the maintenance of existing institutional resources and the creation of new resources; he has ultimate managerial responsibility for a large area of nonacademic activities, he is responsible for public understanding, and by the nature of his office is the chief spokesman of his institution. In these and other areas his work is to plan, to organize, to direct, and to represent. The presidential function should receive the general support of board and faculty.

V. THE ACADEMIC INSTITUTION: THE FACULTY

The faculty has primary responsibility for such fundamental areas as curriculum, subject matter and methods of instruction, research, faculty status, and those aspects of student life which relate to the educational process. On these matters the power of review or final decision lodged in the governing board or delegated by it to the president should be exercised adversely only in exceptional circumstances, and for reasons communicated to the faculty. It is desirable that the faculty should, following such communication, have opportunity for further consideration and further transmittal of its views to the president or board. Budgets, manpower limitations, the time element and the policies of other groups, bodies and agencies having jurisdiction over the institution may set limits to realization of faculty advice.

The faculty sets the requirements for the degrees offered in course, determines when the requirements have been met, and authorizes the president and board to grant the degrees thus achieved.

Faculty status and related matters are primarily a faculty responsibility; this area includes appointments, reappointments, decisions not to reappoint, promotions, the granting of tenure, and dismissal. The primary responsibility of the faculty for such matters is based upon the fact that its judgment is central to general educational policy. Furthermore, scholars in a particular field or activity have the chief competence for judging the work of their colleagues; in such competence it is implicit that responsibility exists for both adverse and favorable judgments. Likewise there is the more general competence of experienced faculty personnel committees having a broader charge. Determinations in these matters should first be by faculty action through established procedures, reviewed by the chief academic officers with the concurrence of the board. The governing board and president should, on questions of faculty status, as in other matters where the faculty has primary responsibility, concur with the faculty judgment except in rare instances and for compelling reasons which should be stated in detail.

The faculty should actively participate in the determination of policies and procedures governing salary increases.

The chairman or head of a department, who serves as the chief representative of his department within an institution, should be selected either by departmental election or by appointment following consultation with members of the department and of related departments; appointments should normally be in conformity with department members' judgment. The chairman or department head should not have tenure in his office; his tenure as a faculty member is a matter of separate right. He should serve for a stated term but without prejudice to re-election or to reappointment by procedures which involve appropriate faculty consultation. Board, administration, and faculty should all bear in mind that the department chairman has a special obligation to build a department strong in scholarship and teaching capacity.

Agencies for faculty participation in the government of the college or university should be established at each level where faculty responsibility is present. An agency should exist for the presentation of the views of the whole faculty. The structure and procedures for faculty participation should be designed, approved, and established by joint action of the components of the institution. Faculty representatives should be selected by the faculty according to procedures determined by the faculty.

The agencies may consist of meetings of all faculty members of a department, school, college, division or university system, or may take the form of faculty-elected executive committees in departments and schools and a faculty-elected senate or council for larger divisions or the institution as a whole.

Among the means of communication among the faculty, administration, and governing board now in use are: (1) circulation of memoranda and reports by board committees, the administration, and faculty committees, (2) joint *ad hoc* committees, (3) standing liaison committees, (4) membership of faculty members on administrative bodies, and (5) membership of faculty members on governing boards. Whatever the channels of communication, they should be clearly understood and observed.

ON STUDENT STATUS

When students in American colleges and universities desire to participate responsibly in the government of the institution they attend, their wish should be recognized as a claim to opportunity both for educational experience and for involvement in the affairs of their college or university. Ways

175

should be found to permit significant student participation within the limits of attainable effectiveness. The obstacles to such participation are large and should not be minimized: inexperience, untested capacity, a transitory status which means that present action does not carry with it subsequent responsibility, and the inescapable fact that the other components of the institution are in a position of judgment over the students. It is important to recognize that student needs are strongly related to educational experience, both formal and informal. Students expect, and have a right to expect, that the educational process will be structured, that they will be stimulated by it to become independent adults, and that they will have effectively transmitted to them the cultural heritage of the larger society. If institutional support is to have its fullest possible meaning it should incorporate the strength, freshness of view and idealism of the student body.

The respect of students for their college or university can be enhanced if they are given at least these opportunities: (1) to be listened to in the classroom without fear of institutional reprisal for the substance of their views, (2) freedom to discuss questions of institutional policy and operation, (3) the right to academic due process when charged with serious violations of institutional regulations, and (4) the same right to hear speakers of their own choice as is enjoyed by other components of the institution.

AAUP DRAFT STATEMENT ON STUDENT PARTICIPATION IN COLLEGE AND UNIVERSITY GOVERNMENT

The 1966 Statement on Government of Colleges and Universities[1] refers to students as "an institutional component coordinate in importance with trustees, administrators, and faculty," notes that "students do not in fact presently have a significant voice in the government of colleges and universities," and expresses the hope that the educational community will "turn its attention to an important need."

The Statement which appears below has been prepared by Committee T on College and University Government, and has been approved by the Committee and the Association's Council for publication in the AAUP *Bulletin. The Association elicits reactions from its members, chapters, and conferences, as well as other interested parties, for this version is only a provisional approach to a complex subject.*

* * * *

INTRODUCTION

The purpose of this Statement is to define the principles and identify several appropriate areas of student participation in the government of colleges and universities. The Statement itself is based on the premise that

---

[1]Jointly formulated by the American Association of University Professors, the American Council on Education, and the Association of Governing Boards of Universities and Colleges. The AAUP approved the Statement at its Fifty-third Annual Meeting in April, 1967; the ACE and AGB have commended it to their member institutions and boards.

Other statements deal with the protections due the individual student or faculty member: the 1940 *Statement of Principles on Academic Freedom and Tenure,* the 1958 *Statement on Procedural Standards in Faculty Dismissal Proceedings* (the basic policy statements, formulated and adopted by the American Association of University Professors and the Association of American Colleges, relating to academic freedom, tenure, and academic due process); the 1968 *Joint Statement on Rights and Freedoms of Students,* approved by the American Association of University Professors, U. S. National Student Association, Association of American Colleges, National Association of Student Personnel Administrators, and National Association of Women Deans and Counselors.

Reprinted from the AAUP *Bulletin, Spring, 1970, pp. 33-35, with permission of the American Association of University Professors.*

students as members of the academic community, in addition to their rights as set forth in the *Joint Statement on Rights and Freedoms of Students,* have a distinctive role which, in respects stated below, qualifies them to share in the exercise of responsible authority on campus; the exercise of that authority is part of their education. Furthermore, there is a greater likelihood of responsible student involvement when students participate in institutional decisions through orderly processes and to the degree appropriate in particular circumstances.

Most importantly, joint effort among all groups in the institution—students, faculty, administration, and governing board—is a prerequisite of sound academic government. A further prerequisite is that all must see themselves as custodians of academic freedom. Like any other group, students should have a voice, sometimes the predominant voice, in decisions which affect them, and their opinions should be regularly solicited even in those areas in which they hold a secondary interest. But academic government depends on more than the accommodation of diverse interests. Joint effort, to be effective, must be rooted in the concept of shared authority. The exercise of shared authority in college and university government, like the protection of academic freedom, requires tolerance, respect, and a sense of community which arises from participation in a common enterprise. The exact mode and extent of student participation depend on conditions which vary from one institution to another; but whatever the area of participation or the form it assumes, the need for cooperation among all groups is inescapable.

STUDENT PARTICIPATION IN ACADEMIC AFFAIRS

The rights of students to free inquiry and expression in the classroom and in conference is asserted in the *Joint Statement on Rights and Freedoms of Students.* Students also have a stake in the quality of their formal education, which must take into account their needs and desires. The categories which follow are those in which student involvement is commonly found; they are not intended to exclude other areas of involvement, which might be developed where there is sufficient student interest. It is for the particular institution to determine the mode and extent of student involvement and the criteria of eligibility for that involvement.

A. Admissions

Students have a stake in the size, composition, and quality of the student body, and should have their views on admissions heard along with those of faculty and administration. Similarly, graduate students should be able to participate constructively in decisions regarding the admissions policy of their respective departments.

B. Academic Programs

Students should be consulted in decisions regarding the development of already-existing programs and the establishment of new programs. As members of the academic community they should have the opportunity for similar involvement with respect to course load and degree requirements. For example, they may submit reports to the administration or the appropriate faculty or departmental committees through their own curriculum committees, or through membership in joint curriculum committees. When provision is made for an experimental student-operated curriculum, students should have primary responsibility for decision-making.[2] When provision is made for student participation in curricular decisions, criteria for eligibility should be devised jointly by faculty and students.

C. Academic Courses and Staff

Students should have the opportunity, through established institutional mechanisms, to assess the value of a course to them, and to make suggestions as to its direction. Students should also be able to express their views on the form and conduct of a class which they have taken, for example through an evaluative questionnaire prepared by joint faculty-student effort, and their opinions should be weighed in faculty decisions affecting faculty status. The faculty member, of course, should be duly protected from capricious and uninformed judgment by students, just as he should be from such judgment by anyone else.

D. Academic Evaluation

The method by which students are evaluated is properly of concern to them. Accordingly, students should be heard with respect to the grading system at an institution. They should also have clearly established means of recourse against prejudiced or capricious grading.

E. Academic Environment

The scheduling of courses, class size, distribution of night and day classes, calendar arrangements, library policy and development, and similar academic arrangements and services affect the ability of students to do academic work. They should share in the formation of policies on these matters.

STUDENT PARTICIPATION
IN OTHER INSTITUTIONAL AFFAIRS

A. Extracurricular Activities

Students should have primary responsibility for activities sponsored by the student body. Other appropriate persons and groups should be able to discuss such activities and be consulted with respect to them. Among these

---

[2]By "primary responsibility" is meant the ability to take action which has the force of legislation and can be over-ruled only in rare instances and for compelling reasons stated in detail.

179

activities are cultural programs sponsored by the student body, student political affairs, and student publications; the intellectual vitality and academic freedom of the student body will be insured in such activities by adequate representation of student taste and opinion.

B. Student Regulations

Students should have primary responsibility for the formulation of clear and readily available regulations pertaining to their personal lives, subject only to such restrictions as may be imposed by law.

C. Student Discipline

Students should have the opportunity to participate in establishing standards and procedures which govern student discipline, and take part also in the actual disciplinary process. Disciplinary proceedings should be in accordance with the provisions of the *Joint Statement on Rights and Freedoms of Students.*

D. Other Institutional Concerns

Students have a right to be heard, through formal means, on questions involving an institution's budget, its physical resources, and its relationship with groups or agencies external to the campus. Provisions should exist for the transmission of student views on such matters to the faculty, president, and governing board.

IMPLEMENTATION

The implementation of the above principles is properly subject to innumerable local variations. On students themselves falls the difficult task of assuring that the diversity of student interests and opinions is adequately represented. All individuals and groups at an institution should support the development of appropriate forms of student participation by assuring that organizations purporting to represent student interests possess a mandate from a clearly defined electorate, are accountable to that electorate, and function through orderly procedures agreed upon through joint action by students and the other members of the academic community. Student representatives, like other representatives in any area of university government, should be free to vote according to their best judgment. At all times, students should enjoy protection from the exercise of tyranny by a majority or a minority, the right to petition for and be granted an open hearing on a question of student rights or student participation, and the right of access—both to information on institutional government and to grievance procedures for complaints relating to their life in and out of the classroom.

Limits on participation by students may be dictated in some instances, such as those in which a violation of law or of confidentiality might result. Where any limitation exists, the student should have the right to challenge it in a manner consistent with legality and the principles of academic freedom. All forms of participation in the government of the institution should be so devised as to preserve the academic freedom to which all groups are equally entitled.

Student involvement in institutional government may include membership—voting and nonvoting—on departmental committees, on college or division councils and committees, or on the university senate or any other principal legislative body and its committees. Where they do not hold membership on these bodies, students should be able to place matters for action on their agendas and to receive a prompt report on the disposition of those matters. Student opinion should also be consulted, where feasible, in the selection of presidents, chief academic and nonacademic administrative officers including the dean of students, and faculty. Sometimes separate and parallel student structures are desired in place of or in addition to mixed bodies. Where this is the case, care should be taken to guarantee that the student bodies not function merely as subordinate entities subject to arbitrary veto by faculty or administrative groups, and that all groups enjoy meaningful channels of appeal. The procedure for election or appointment of students to duly constituted instruments of student participation should be developed in consultation with all directly concerned persons and groups. It should be made available as information to the entire campus community, and be reviewed periodically.

Meaningful participation in college and university government is not guaranteed merely by the presence of students on committees; in some cases, indeed, this may inhibit free student expression. Such expression may well play an important role in institutional affairs through the campus newspaper, published evaluations of courses, or discussion programs on the state of the institutions which bring different constituencies together. In any case, the informal exchange of opinion, like the formal participation in the processes of institutional government, should involve students, faculty, administration, and governing board in a continuing joint effort.